LAW *and* PEACE

LAW *and* PEACE

By

EDWIN D. DICKINSON

Philadelphia
UNIVERSITY OF PENNSYLVANIA PRESS
1951

Manufactured in the United States of America

For

M. H. D.

Acknowledgments

The author is indebted to The Foundation Press, Inc., Brooklyn, N. Y., for permission to make liberal use in the first of these essays of the substance and much of the form of what appears as an editorial note on "The Factual Bases of International Behavior" in a book entitled *Cases and Materials on International Law* published recently by The Foundation Press in its University Casebook Series. The author is similarly indebted to the publishers of the *California Law Review*, Berkeley, California, for permission to make comparable use in the second of these essays of "International Law: An Inventory," appearing in the *California Law Review's* issue of December, 1945 (Volume XXXIII, pp. 506-42).

Contents

Foreword

These essays are a record or report of four lectures delivered at Northwestern University in February 1950, on the Norman Wait Harris Foundation, under the general title "Law and Peace." They present results of an inquiry which has been in progress for a number of years and which has ranged over wide areas. Our world has perhaps two and a quarter billion inhabitants living in varying stages of what we choose to call civilization. Apparently all or most of its inhabitants want peace. What has law to contribute to the realization of this vague but widespread aspiration? What has law to do with peace?

The general title is the product of a bit of personal history which may be of interest. When first initiated the project was to be called "Peace under Law." It was not long, however, before inquiry's progress had largely discredited this initial formulation. There was so much to remind one of what every lawyer should know that Law provides no cure-all or panacea. Thus it is vain to hope that a troubled world may be saved from its torment by superimposing codes or constitutions. A title suggesting the hope was misleading and had to be discarded. The next formulation was "Law under Peace." This was adopted tentatively about the time that spadework for the first and second essays was being completed. In retrospect it must be conceded that it was quite as far from reality in the other direction. It is true that Law is no panacea, but neither is it a mere recording for political statecraft in search of order on this turbulent planet. Law has statecraft of its own. And so another formulation came to be rejected. The third and final formulation was "Law and Peace," the title under which the essays are now published. Let it be noted that the final title was no soft-spoken compromise. If there was less of commitment in it than in the formulations previously rejected, there were also significant implications. Law in relation to Peace might occupy a great segment of the far-flung front in the everlasting struggle of humanity against unreason. It might be found to have vast potentialities as yet unexploited. It might . . . but first evidence and the argument. There will be a time then for conclusions.

LAW *and* PEACE

The Community of Nations

I

WHILE THERE are many trends toward world community in the increasing interdependence of the world's peoples, there is nothing more embracing in the way of governmental organization at the present time than an imperfectly coördinated society of separate states. There are approximately fourscore such states or nations in the world of our day. Sixty, as we write, are members of the United Nations. Others remain without, for varying reasons, hoping ultimately to be brought within. The community of these nations, including both those inside and those outside the United Nations, is the community of international law. The adjective "international" has no doubt suggested as much. What sort of community or society is this with which we are thus presented at the threshold of our inquiry?

Speaking generally, it is apparent that the community of nations is a community extraordinary, wholly unique, and admitting of no simple explanation by recourse to analogies or to the familiar formulae of lawyers' over-simplifications. Indeed, if we are to achieve a minimum of understanding, we shall be obliged to put aside at the outset some of the lawyer's traditional amenities and look at nations undressed. What are they basically? Why do they behave in community as they do? What are the principal factors which condition their response to a regime of order? That they are real bodies, we know, shaped in the confines of a living space, supported by resources and productivity, animated by culture and tradition and correspondingly affected as regards notions of justice or right. There are features which clearly require a closer scrutiny. They may have more to do with order or the lack of it than is sometimes appreciated.

II

The first feature which impresses as we proceed to view the community of nations is the complexity of the distribution among its members of the earth's inhabitable surface. The lines of division or boundary present an intricacy which is explicable only by reference to geography and history. The bounds may be set by seas, mountains, rivers, or deserts, or at artificial lines which have been accepted for a variety of reasons. Here one discovery or migration has sometime met another, and a line of compromise has been established. There a line may have been fixed in concert or conference to add assurance to balance of power. Here an army stood, a fort was built, or an invasion spent its force in times when communication was slow and supply lines short. There a settlement was made or a way of communication or natural resource reserved for national advantage. Needless to say, there are frontiers which no longer retain their original significance but which have been preserved in deference to the inertia which opposes unsettlement, to national pride, or to other considerations. So the jigsaw puzzle stands, with infrequent adjustments, at once consequence and cause of important rivalries of interest and national policy.

Moreover it is neither desirable nor possible that these rivalries of interest be wholly divorced from law. They are stuff of which legal adjustment and the ensuing order must be made. Thus the nation whose lands are divided as are those of Pakistan or Panama must have problems and an outlook unlike the problems and outlook of another country where the homeland is firmly united. Thus, also, the island nation may see problems of sea law in perspective quite different from that of an inland country. Canada and the Soviet Union, whose lands sprawl most of the way across the approaches to the Arctic, may be content to settle problems of control in this vital area on principles of contiguity applied in sectors, but we may be assured that neither Norway nor the United States will regard this as a satisfactory basis of accommodation. Without further example, we may proceed in confidence that geography has something basic to contribute to the development of law and that here, as elsewhere, good law will be neither all of one approach nor of another. It will be a reconciliation of interests as variant as those of Pakistan and India, Switzerland and Britain, or Norway and Canada.

Perhaps few of the geographic complexities have been more troublesome over the years than the vast and complicated disparities which are so imperfectly suggested in the aphorism that there are great states and small. In truth, there are nations of every resource, shape, and size. There are diminutive nations: Luxembourg, smaller than Rhode Island; Lebanon, smaller than Connecticut; Israel, Albania, Haiti, and Belgium, each smaller than the combined areas of Maryland and Delaware; and Salvador, Switzerland, and Denmark, each smaller than the combined areas of Massachusetts and New Hampshire. There are nations which have been able to occupy and hold, through a combination of more or less fortuitous circumstances, a little more of the earth's inhabitable surface: Austria, Ceylon, Costa Rica, the Dominican Republic, and Ireland, each smaller than Maine; Hungary, Iceland, Jordan, and Panama, each smaller than Ohio; Bulgaria, Cuba, Greece, Guatemala, Honduras, and Liberia, each smaller than Alabama; and Czechoslovakia, Nicaragua, Syria, and Uruguay, each smaller than South Dakota. Of the nations which reckon their lands at one hundred thousand square miles or more, Finland, Germany, Iraq, Italy, Japan, New Zealand, Norway, Paraguay, the Philippines, and Poland are substantially smaller than California; and Afghanistan, Burma, Ecuador, Spain, Sweden, and Thailand are smaller than Texas. Included in the list of those larger than Texas and in some instances roughly comparable to Texas and California combined are Bolivia, Colombia, Egypt, Ethiopia, Iran, Pakistan, Peru, Saudi Arabia, Turkey, the Union of South Africa, and Venezuela. Indonesia and Mexico each claim approximately three quarters of a million square miles. Controlling more than a million square miles of the good earth are Argentina, just over the million mark; India, about a million and a quarter; Australia, nearly three million; Brazil, more than three and a quarter millions; Canada, nearly three and a half millions; China and the United States, each more than three and a half millions; the British Empire, excluding the commonwealths, perhaps four millions;

France, including the overseas empire, well over four millions; Russia, in round numbers, eight millions, or approximately one-sixth of the earth's landed surface; and the British Empire, together with the commonwealths, nearly one-fourth of the earth's landed surface. It should be noted also that there are nations essentially diminutive or small which have succeeded in holding on sufferance and for prolonged periods extensive colonial empires. Such has been the case with The Netherlands and Portugal.

While we have learned long since that influence is not necessarily in proportion to area and that in shifting connotation small nations may be great or great nations small, we have also learned that these disparities among the national homelands have marked indelibly and inevitably the law which has been developed within the international community. It is enough to remind at this point of the extraordinary emphasis upon sovereignty and the equality of states which has so long dominated international legal thinking, of the well-nigh insuperable obstacles with which such thinking appeared at one time to obstruct the way to organized international coöperation, and of the formulae or principles which have since been developed with respect to contribution, representation, voting, and the like in international organs. It was not so long ago that a very small republic would have no part in any international court unless assured of as many judges on the court as any other nation. It was in the same debates, if memory serves, that a Chinese delegate blandly suggested judicial representation in proportion to population! A generation passed, and two wars, while rivalries and fears resulting so largely from the disparate distribution of living space were reconciled somewhat in a more useful development of law.

III

The next feature to invite comment and excite the imagination is the extraordinary diversity of national situations with respect to matters of locale, climate, and natural resource. We have mentioned a variance of outlook on policy and law as between island and inland nations. Britain, Cuba, Iceland, Japan, and the Philippines are island countries whose people look in all directions to the sea. Afghanistan, Austria, Bolivia, Czechoslovakia, Hungary, Paraguay, and Switzerland are landlocked with corresponding constraint of interest and aspiration. Some nations are situated on or near great international rivers, historic arteries of communication and commerce, as are the countries of Central Europe, of the Balkans, or of the region in South America drained by the great river system which debouches through the Rio de la Plata. Others, as Brazil, China, Egypt, or the United States, control largely their principal watercourses. There are nations, such as Albania, Norway, or Switzerland, whose locations are mountainous to the point of rendering large areas uninhabitable, or at least of a nature to tax severely the rugged virtues of those who struggle to inhabit. There are others, as Belgium, Denmark, Hungary, or Paraguay, whose homelands are largely lowland and rich in fertile plain. Some nations, as Canada, Finland, Norway, Russia, and Sweden, have been conditioned to a degree by the rigors of an arctic or subarctic climate and have developed interests and proficiencies which correspond. Others lie on or near the equator and have been conditioned naturally, as regards interests and proficiencies, by the tropic's heat. Iceland and Ecuador, each named for its locale, represent the extremes as well as any. There are countries of heavy rainfall and abundant vegetation—Liberia, the Philippines, or Thailand—and others of vast aridity and inhospitable desert—Egypt, Iraq, or Saudi Arabia. Thus Egypt on the map lays claim to an area greater than that of our three Pacific Coast states combined, but in all its vast expanse of sand and stone only the ribbon-like valley of the Nile, the Nile delta, and a few oases, comprising an area less than one-third that of Ohio, are habitable. In some countries there are few climatic extremes, while in others meteorology makes a sport of variation.

The diversities of natural resource are even more impressive and more impelling in the immediacy of their impact upon policy and law than locale and climate. For more than a century, coal and iron and other metals have come increasingly to be recognized as providing the essential bases of national prosperity and influence. More recently the control of petroleum resources has become an open sesame to national riches. Some nations have had these things in balanced abundance, while others have had them in part, in negligible quantities, or not at all. It is no coincidence that hegemony has passed to such countries as Britain, Russia, or the United States, where basic resources have been ample, or that lands such as Iran, Iraq, Mexico, Peru, Rumania, Saudi Arabia, or Venezuela, having petroleum unbalanced by other bases of a well-rounded development, have become the objects of an officious solicitude on the part of nations in need of oil.

We shall have more to say presently of industrialization and of a resulting dependency upon imports of the raw materials of manufacture and the foodstuffs for workers. Only a few nations have had the resources to industrialize in relative balance. Most have had increasingly to look abroad for raw materials, foodstuffs, or both. At the same time other nations have come to depend for their very livelihood upon raw material or foodstuff exports. There are a few, indeed, where the economy and corresponding national policy have come to converge upon the export of a single product or crop. In Bolivia governments rise or fall on the price of tin, in Cuba on the price of sugar. The banana has long been the key to prosperity or depression in Honduras. In Iceland the lowly fish is king.

By all the tests which have been found reliable hitherto, there are nations now of an intermediate influence whose unexploited resources may contain the promise of a significant expansion of prosperity and power. Such, no doubt, are Australia, where rainfall and climate must be reckoned as restraining factors, or Brazil, where account must be taken of meager resources of coal and oil and the unsolved riddle of the great basin of the Amazon, or Canada, where limitations are implicit in the vast expanse of its frozen northland, or ancient China and emerging India, where more material progress must wait upon the achievement of a minimum of political order and stability. Among relatively smaller or less populous countries, where natural resources are at hand in quantity and balance sufficient to encourage further exploitation, there may be in prospect less of dependency, more of prosperity, and a corresponding expansion of influence. As much may be forecast cautiously and in varying degree for Chile, Poland, the Union of South Africa, or Yugoslavia. Where important natural resources appear to be largely lacking or available only in negligible supply, the forecast presumably should be more restrained. So perhaps of Argentina, notwithstanding its agricultural richness, or of Italy, notwithstanding its historic past, or of New Zealand, notwithstanding the beauty of its land and the progressive enlightenment of its people. As regards other nations, any attempt at forecast must be hedged about by a multiplicity of reservations, except perhaps to say of a very considerable number that they are too obviously restricted as regards location, climate, or natural resource to enjoy measurable prospect of improved material influence.

Needless to say, in these notes upon the distribution of natural resources no attempt has been made to forecast the effects of progress in the development of atomic energy. The effects may be profoundly unsettling throughout the world. Some resources may come to have less of relative importance, while others may acquire a new and unprecedented significance. It may be that new criteria of material influence will be forced upon us and that the rise and decline of nations will be gauged in the future with reference to the control or use of atomic power. Clearly new forces are in the making and the speed of change is certain to be accelerated. The basic problems, however, will probably continue to be presented in familiar patterns. Our knowledge of nuclear physics may become even more terrifyingly destructive, but there is no real prospect as yet that it will become the means of expanding our lands, drying up our seas, or tempering the rigors of the arctic or the heat of the tropic sun. Presumably man will continue a surface dwelling creature who takes his living initially from the earth and the sea. And presumably the intricacy of the earth's livable surface and the maladjustment of its riches among the earth's peoples will continue to condition national policies with respect to important international problems. For the time being, at least, one of the most striking consequences of recourse to atomic energy has been to greatly accentuate among nations the troublesome disparities of resource and power.

It will not be doubted that these factors of locale, climate, and natural resource contribute to the determination of national outlook and policy. Patently they must also condition the national approach to problems of law. They are among the things of which such problems are made and are factors which must be weighed and weighed again in the continuing processes of accommodation. It will not be too difficult to anticipate, for example, important national views with respect to the law of shipping, privileges of land transit, the regimes of rivers, the polar regions, coöperation in overcoming tropical disease, access to oil or the ores of uranium, or the distribution of rice, rubber, or wheat surpluses. It may be much more difficult to find tolerable bases of reconciliation, but surely the difficulties will not ordinarily be made less by substituting juristic fiction for physical fact. Jurists no less than statesmen must needs regard Argentina in relation to its pampas, Brazil with reference to its Amazon, Britain in awareness of its far-flung empire and corresponding dependence upon the seven seas, Chile in understanding of its remoteness, its unusual configuration, and its diversities of climate, Egypt in terms of its dependence upon the Nile, Saudi Arabia in appraisement of the resources of its desert, Switzerland in understanding of its mountainous isolation, or Turkey in comprehension of its Straits at the crossroads of empire. These are examples noted only to point up again the interdependence among nations of the factual bases of their national life and the development of an international law.

IV

The third feature to challenge understanding, as we endeavor to comprehend basic national reactions to an international regime of order, is the feature of populations. Into the varied lands, adjusting to locale, climate, and resource, have moved peoples in varying numbers, congested in or sparsely scattered over habitable areas, and of diverse colors, cultures, and characteristics. The interaction has been reciprocal. The land has conditioned the people. The people have given character to the land. The ensuing conflicts of policy, described loosely as problems of population, have become inseparable in international relations from corresponding conflicts in the law.

At the outset we are confronted by vast disparities of numbers which are bound to have more than a mere statistical significance. We may begin again with such diminutive countries as Costa Rica, Iceland, Jordan, Luxembourg, or Panama, each having a total population less than that of the American city of San Francisco, or with the smaller countries, including Albania, Guatemala,

Haiti, Honduras, Liberia, New Zealand, Nicaragua, Norway, Paraguay, Salvador, Saudi Arabia, Syria, and Uruguay, where the total population of each is less than that of the city of Chicago. The list of the nations having in each fewer souls than are counted in the city of New York, as would be anticipated, is comparatively impressive. It includes Australia, Austria, Bolivia, Bulgaria, Chile, Cuba, Denmark, Ethiopia, Greece, Peru, Sweden, and Switzerland. Others may match New York state's total population with a modest margin of more or less—Afghanistan, Argentina, Canada, Czechoslovakia, Egypt, Iran, Thailand, or Yugoslavia—or, in fewer instances, two or three times over—Brazil, Italy, Poland, or Spain. And here again, alongside the diminutive, the small, the medium small, and the large, are the giants among nations where inhabitants are counted at from one hundred to more than four hundred millions—the United States, the Soviet Union, Britain and France, if their empires are included, India and China. So great are the disparities, indeed, that the combined populations of all other nations in the Western Hemisphere are less than that of the United States, and the combined populations of more than half of the nations of the earth are scarcely equivalent to the population of the Soviet Union. Such facts are reflected inevitably and in a wide variety of ways in the formulation of national policies, in national reactions to policies formulated elsewhere, and in the developing processes of legal accommodation.

Important as they are, however, mere numbers are by no means the sole or even the principal key to an understanding of population problems. At this point it becomes necessary to recall the distribution of lands and natural resources. In relation to living space and local means of subsistence, some countries are heavily or excessively populated. Such has been and in many instances continues to be conspicuously true of Albania, Belgium, Britain, China, Egypt, Germany, Greece, India, Ireland, Italy, Japan, The Netherlands, or Norway. Some, as Belgium or The Netherlands, have found partial solution in a skillful and intensive exploitation. Others, as China or India, have been the victims of recurring famines or, as China, Germany, Greece, or Italy, have been consistent exporters of men. In any case such nations are not hospitable to immigration, are likely to become countries of emigration, and are prone to corresponding political and legal predilections. On the other side there are underpopulated countries such as Argentina, Australia, Bolivia, Brazil, Canada, Chile, Colombia, Costa Rica, New Zealand, or Venezuela. Countries so situated are likely to provide regions for immigration, or at least to be viewed with a jaundiced eye by the more crowded peoples, and their fixations will naturally be shaped accordingly. Rising barriers to immigration in one part of the world result in an augmented pressure upon the livable lands of another, as in many of the countries of southern and eastern Europe, and over all there impends the extraordinary concentration in southeast Asia and nearby insular countries, constituting about twenty per cent of the earth's landed surface, of nearly one-half of the world's present population. These are but suggestions of the importance for policy and law of the density or sparsity of population in relation to national resources.

So much for numbers and their distribution, which together carry us only to the threshold of understanding.

Beyond the threshold we encounter the baffling problems of race and color. The races of man are black, white, yellow, red, or brown or, in some parts of the earth, a blending of the primary racial hues. Perhaps a third of the earth's peoples are white and two-thirds colored. Even among the varicolored or the white there are further racial divisions. Chinese of north and south are dissimilar. The nations of India are a racial hodgepodge, as contemporary events so sharply remind us. Polynesian, Malaysian, Indian, or African are oversimplifications. White peoples may be of Celtic, Teutonic, Latin, or Slavonic origins, to mention only the better known and familiar. Over all and pervading all, nurtured and complicated by a variety of forces, is that elusive thing commonly described as racial prejudice.

The population movements of history have poured racial colors over the earth in bewildering confusion to enrich the soils of discord. It is almost as though some malignant spirit had spattered his colors deliberately to confound the hard-won amenities of man. Australia has come by rigorous exclusion to be called a white man's continent. Europe and most of North America are predominantly white. Central and South America are white and red with a splash of yellow and black. Asia and its environs are partly white, more largely brown, but predominantly yellow. Indonesia is brown, but with substantial intrusions of white or yellow, and even a little black. Africa is white and brown but predominantly black.

Regional or continental color distributions, moreover, are hardly suggestive of the race problems which perplex particular nations. There are nations with colored or uncolored minorities and others without them. In New

Zealand the Polynesian minority is reconciled and respected. In South Africa, on the other hand, a white minority rules over a nation that is predominantly black and the color problem pervades every aspect of the national life. The United States has a black minority, constituting approximately one-tenth of its population and concentrated heavily in the states of the old south, which is the source of an acute color problem as yet unsolved. Of the Latin American countries, a few are predominantly white, whether by absorption of the native races, as in Chile, or by extermination, as in Argentina; others are largely Indian but are ruled precariously by a white or mixed minority; and still others are predominantly Indian in basic temperament and outlook. Cuba has an important black minority; Haiti is all black; and Brazil is a potpourri of white and red and black, with few color lines, and thus far committed somewhat successfully to the repudiation of color consciousness and discrimination. Of the one-color nations, a few have suffered from a megalomania of color superiority, others have been made color conscious by resistance or discrimination elsewhere, and some have been happily spared either inferiority complexes or delusions of grandeur. In the Soviet Union, it would appear, the invidious color line has been largely eliminated by fiat of an authoritarian government.

In a world in which the white peoples have enjoyed hitherto a none too tolerant ascendancy, yet one in which the colored peoples predominate numerically and have been aroused increasingly by the stirrings of nationalism and the urge for ampler recognition, these things are of tremendous import. In the Arab lands, in Burma, China, India, and Indonesia the "white man's burden" is demanding a long delayed opportunity to walk alone. Similar adjustments are in the making throughout Africa and elsewhere in the world. The adjustments may be difficult, but certain it is that the arrogance of empires must be tempered increasingly by tolerance and understanding and that influence must pass increasingly to those peoples which are successful in the cultivation of tolerance and understanding both at home and abroad.

How much these things have channeled the development of international law, and the extent to which they have sometimes prevented any useful development, are matters too well understood to require an extensive illustration. Population disparities, like disparities of area and resource, have long retarded and more recently given significant direction to the law of international organization. Population density in relation to resources has had a deal to do inevitably with the growth of law and practice concerning the exclusion, admission, expulsion, protection, and naturalization of aliens. It has also had an important effect upon nationality laws, conflicts among nationality laws, and the protection of nationals abroad. As is well known, there remain in consequence of diverging policies many and important gaps which the law has not yet been able to bridge. How much law has been similarly shaped or frustrated by color consciousness it would perhaps be difficult to say. Certainly there are problems of discrimination not otherwise wholly explicable. Certainly the contemporary effort to promote and encourage respect for human rights and fundamental freedoms for all "without distinction of any kind" as regards race or color must meet such consciousness head on. Even these conflicts are not beyond reconciliation although, deeply rooted in race, location, and culture, they are of a kind likely to tax resources of reconciliation to the utmost.

V

The fourth feature to encourage renewed efforts of understanding, initially in the realm of policy and ultimately no less in the realm of law, is something already touched upon in what has been said about locale, climate, and natural resources. Beginning with the land, its location, climate, and resources, add population in adjustment over the years to the riches or poverty which nature has provided, mature in history, and there emerges something which may be loosely described as a national economy. As hitherto suggested, the national economies are complex and varied things, more varied even than the varicolored flags which nations fly as the symbols of their nationhood.

No modern nation is wholly self-sufficient. A few, rich alike in agriculture, mining, and industry, as Czechoslovakia, France, Russia, or the United States, have had the resources to approach a balance which at intervals has suggested self-sufficiency. Actually, however, the approach has been relative and the suggestion largely illusory. Communication and transport and the increasing complexities of modern life have made every nation in varying degree dependent upon its trade with others. Only the hermit nation has been able to escape the trend and among nations the hermit has been generally both backward and poor.

Actually most nations are startlingly dependent, in one way or another, upon continuing exchanges for the goods, services, or materials which others are in a position to supply. The emphasis should be placed upon "one way or another," for the variations are many. In some countries the economy is predominantly agricultural, fabricated goods are largely obtained from abroad, and the nation's reliance is primarily upon foreign markets for the trading of its agricultural surplus. Close the world's markets for wheat, meat, wool, and dairy products and the economies of Argentina, Australia, Denmark, New Zealand, or Uruguay could be well-nigh ruined. Cut off the trade in sugar and tobacco and Cuba would be in the doldrums. While Brazil has riches sufficiently diversified to have escaped somewhat from its former dependence upon exports of coffee, Colombia, Costa Rica, and Guatemala remain heavily dependent upon trade in the fragrant bean. In Costa Rica, Guatemala, and Honduras, similarly, the banana buys a major share of the things that are needed and not produced at home. Finland relies heavily upon the export of timber and its products. In other countries there has been comparable dependence upon the export of metals. Chile has leaned heavily in the past upon copper and nitrates, South Africa upon gold. Bolivia's lopsided dependence upon tin has already been noted. The place of oil in the economies of Iran, Iraq, Saudi Arabia, or Venezuela requires no emphasis. It is common knowledge.

On the other hand, there are countries in considerable number which have become heavily industrialized and populous while in continuing short supply of materials for their mills and food for their workers. These countries must perforce rely upon trading the products of their mills for the raw materials of manufacture and the foods required by their peoples. Such has been conspicuously the case, though in varying degree, in Belgium, Britain, Germany, Japan, and Switzerland. The maritime nation so situated may also be in a position to trade shipping services for materials or food. Some of the smaller countries having unbalanced economies have built or acquired fleets and engaged extensively in the overseas carrying trade, thus improving substantially their economic position. Denmark, Greece, The Netherlands, and Norway have been notable for maritime ventures. Most nations are trading nations of necessity. The bases of necessity vary. So do responses of policy and law to the necessities which the economy presents.

There is another aspect of the trade by which nations live which merits at least passing attention. Whether for reasons of economics, politics, geography, history, or some combination of factors thus suggested, certain nations in the past have become conspicuously the trade dependents of others. Thus, prior to the last great war, Albania was largely dependent upon Italy; other Balkan nations were dependent upon Germany; Belgium, Finland, Ireland, New Zealand, Portugal, and South Africa were dependent upon Britain; and Brazil, Cuba, Honduras, and Mexico were dependent upon the United States. These are examples only. The degree of dependency has varied. The war and its aftermath have upset obviously many of the old relationships. Balkan countries, Middle Europe, and Finland have been swept into an expanded Russian orbit. What other changes may be in process or in prospect in this changing world it is perhaps too early to predict with confidence. Certain it is, however, that national policies and commitments will continue to be largely influenced by the main lines of international trade.

In its impact upon the national economies, indeed, the last great war had devastating and far-reaching effects. Germany and Japan, formerly great industrial and trading nations, were well-nigh destroyed. The empires of the British, the French, and the Dutch were shaken to their very foundations. Russia was badly hurt but emerged with new confidence. China, accustomed to suffering, has continued an economic and political chaos. The United States has discovered a tremendous fighting potential, accumulated a colossal debt, and emerged with the beginnings of a global outlook. Always poor, Albania, Austria, Bulgaria, Finland, Greece, Hungary, and Italy have been further impoverished. Belgium, Czechoslovakia, The Netherlands, Norway, the Philippines, and Poland have been confronted with prodigious problems of reconstruction. Spain still languishes, physically and culturally, in the wake of its disastrous revolution. As always, the victors have suffered with the vanquished. Precisely what the economies of nations will be like a generation or even a decade hence no man may surely know. It is certain only that great changes will have been wrought, that there will be more rather than less of interdependence, that the factual bases of national economic life will be varied as hitherto, and that the reconciling of conflicting interests in adjustments of policy and law will continue to present tasks of complexity and magnitude.

It need not be emphasized that the principles and processes of international reconciliation in these matters are likely to develop usefully only as the factual bases of relevant national behavior are understood. As much must be said, assuredly, of that important and somewhat neglected body of international practice which is recorded chiefly in commercial treaties. As much will be conspicuously true also of such law and practice as may develop about the International Food and Agriculture Organization. So also, if obstacles are eventually overcome, as regards the International Trade Organization. In such relationships it would seem that the development of international law must always be largely a matter of improving and expanding the principles and methods of adjustment among divergent national economies.

VI

As a fifth and final feature in this survey of the factual bases of national behavior, we may group together for convenience the imponderables of polity, culture, and tradition. There is lacking the neat phrase or formula which describes them as an aggregate, though needless to say each is indispensable to an understanding of the others. In their more visible manifestations they find expression in government, social order, and national policy. Less tangibly they combine to produce the ideologies with which nations come to be identified. They tend of course to become as variant as the resources of land, people, and economy from which they spring.

It may come as something of a shock to those for whom the democratic polity is not only a practice but a faith to be reminded that even relative democracy has yet to prove its worth in most nations of the earth. Under varying forms of government, it has been substantially realized in Britain and in several of the members of the

British Commonwealth, in the United States, in France and perhaps seven or eight of the smaller nations of Europe, and in Iceland. Czechoslovakia made a courageous beginning, but has now become perforce of another communion. Austria had an interval of political freedom between the wars, but the late war's aftermath has beclouded its future. Italy is striving valiantly in these postwar years to return to democratic ways. In South America, Uruguay has followed increasingly the way of personal liberty and popular rule, and there has been at least a nascent democracy in Chile. Elsewhere in the Americas there are the forms of free institutions, and there has been much valiant effort to give them substance, but in the outcome the substance has remained more often than otherwise an indigenous kind of authoritarian rule. Elsewhere in Europe, in Asia and in Africa, there have been monarchies and republics, parliaments and elections, but the forms of popular government, where they have been permitted to develop, have been generally little more than a façade for the rule of clique or caste. Portugal and Spain remain up to the present avowedly fascist. Russia exemplifies the communist type of totalitarian regime; and within an expanded Russian orbit, in Europe and Asia, it seems evident that polities must incline toward if they do not wholly surrender to the Russan ideology. In America we may believe firmly that political democracy is on the march, but we may not blink the fact that if a truly democratic polity were put to a vote in the community of nations today it would command no more than a modest minority of sincere support.

The cultures of nations, viewed superficially, appear to have been moulded in fewer patterns. When examined more closely, however, it becomes apparent that they are as diverse as the lands, peoples, and polities which have made them what they are. It could hardly be otherwise, indeed, for the national culture is in each instance history's precipitate of the actions and interactions of all the varied factors which combine to make a nation. Thus we are accustomed to speak loosely of an Anglo-American culture; but clearly this culture is one thing in ancient, crowded, industrialized, seafaring Britain and quite another across the vast expanses of robust, racially mixed, and rising Canada. It is bound to be different from either in the south of Africa, where subtropical lands teem with brown and black dominated by a white minority that is largely of mixed Dutch and French Huguenot descent, or in New Zealand's more salubrious climate, where the white stock is largely derived from group migrations primarily English and the general outlook has become more British than the British. It has developed its own peculiar qualities in remote and white Australia in the South Pacific, and is conspicuously a thing of its own kind in the rich domain and racial melting pot that is called the United States of America.

Similarly, we speak inexactly of a western European or of an eastern European culture, though Latin, Teuton, Scandinavian, and Slav have developed over the centuries, each in their own place and time, an enlightenment of varying emphases and refinements. The Balkans and the Near East are a cultural hodgepodge. Asia to most Westerners remains a continent of infinite mystery. In Africa, the ancient and the modern, relative maturity and the extreme primitive, are found side by side. Central and South America, often thought of popularly as areas of common cultural characteristics, are actually areas of significant diversities. Thus Costa Ricans are predominantly white, of Spanish cultural origins and highly literate, while Guatemalans are predominantly Indian, live in cultural isolation, and are highly illiterate. The Dominican Republic is largely white and traditionally Spanish, while neighboring Haiti is peopled by the black race and is French in its cultural heritage. A native form of Portuguese is spoken in Brazil, of Spanish in Argentina, and cultures differing substantially from either the Portuguese or Spanish are being fused in each. Notwithstanding the familiar similarities, none of these nations are peas in a pod. Moreover their diversities are at present becoming more, rather than less, noteworthy.

Variations among national cultures have been fostered or strongly fortified by diversities of language and literature, in many parts of the world by differences of religion, and throughout most of the world by the rising tide of nationalism which has been so characteristic of the century and a half following the French Revolution. Language obstructions to understanding and accord have been fundamental, nor have ingenious attempts to resolve the babel been more than flecks upon the surface of the deeper stream. As regards religion, there has been happily a decline of fanaticism, though there are still nations strongly Catholic, others predominantly Protestant, others traditionally Buddhist, and a few that are zealously Mohammedan. In the nations of India religion affects every phase of life, and religious conflicts, particularly between Hindu and Moslem, have retarded greatly the national emergence which is now in progress. Although it may be a passing mood, there have been a few countries of late in which the dominant political cult has come near to making a religion of irreligion.

As religious fanaticism has waned throughout most of the world, something akin to political fanaticism has arisen to take its place. Compounded of the hopes and fears of peoples, and rationalized by political philosophers long dead, a pride of land, race, and culture has come to be expressed increasingly in ardent and at times irrational insistence upon liberty without responsibility. In the realm of ideas, national sovereignty has become one of the strongest bulwarks of cultural parochialism.

There is at least one incident of all this that has been particularly persistent and troublesome. As a consequence of the casual pouring of populations into variant areas, many nations have come to have cultural, linguistic, religious, or racial minorities in their midst. A cultural minority of quality should, and frequently does, enrich the national culture. Where there is toleration the enrichment may proceed unimpeded. Unhappily, however, the enrichment is not always appreciated and there are peoples prone to intolerance with resulting discriminations and discords. To other cultural variances in the minority, add an alien language and the obstacles to mutual understanding are increased with corresponding increase in the probability of discords. To general cultural and language differences, add a notable divergence in religious faith, particularly in a country where the prevailing religious preference is strongly held, and the temptations to enforced assimilation are multiplied. Add racial differences, or the minority's residual loyalty to the nation of its principal cultural affiliations, and the situation is overripe for repression and strife. Thus so-called cultural minorities may be compounded of various elements, may, and too often do, overtax the limits of local toleration, and may become the objects of discrimination, enforced assimilation, or in extreme cases, of extermination. Compatriots elsewhere are correspondingly aroused and the minorities problem becomes a fertile source of international dissension. Cultural minorities are more than a problem. They are firm reminders, if reminders are needed, of the fundamental importance of cultural factors in contemporary international relations.

It is sometimes urged that communication, travel, trade, and an expanding exchange in the realms of art, science, and invention may tend progressively to level cultural diversities among the nations. Coöperation in education is advanced as the best assurance of an effective political coöperation. There is a core of important truth in the notion, but unfortunately it has other implications which are sometimes misleading. True it is that French has long been the international language of diplomacy, that English has become largely the international language of commerce, that maritime nations have found an extensive accord in the customs and agreements of the sea, that the qualities of Dutch or Italian painting are a heritage of all mankind, or that the structure of the atom is the same in Russia and in the United States. The actual leavening has been superficial thus far, however, and there is no assurance that it will be more than superficial for some time to come. Moreover it is unsafe to assume that understanding and affection are synonymous, or that comprehension is necessarily followed by conscious or unconscious imitation. Reactions to comprehension may be quite the contrary. We cannot forecast with assurance what the

Slav will do with American industrial machines, or the Chinese with Western political ideas, or the Arab with oil and the salvage of empire. Cultural differences are deeply rooted in land, race, and history. It is entirely possible that they may be confirmed and fortified, in important respects, by expanded cultural exchanges.

In any event we shall not erase soon important variances of tradition and national sensitivity. The very antiquity of his national culture has meaning for the thoughtful Chinese or Egyptian. There is latent always in the Greek or the Italian a pride in the historic greatness of his land. The outlook of the informed Spaniard is conditioned substantially by the empire of his forebears, of the Briton or Frenchman by the empire of which he is presently a part. The seas are life itself to Briton, Dutchman, or Norwegian. The lights of his capital are a beacon of national tradition to Austrian or Frenchman. No understanding Belgian is likely to forget that his country has been the cockpit of Europe, or Frenchman that his land has been three times invaded in as many generations, or Pole that his country has been ruthlessly partitioned by its neighbors. The Swiss is characteristically jealous of his isolated neutrality, and the Ottoman of his Straits. The Irishman, the Czechoslovakian, or the American of either continent will remember a prolonged struggle for freedom, the Russian his great land unwashed by friendly seas, the miseries of his people, the triumph of revolution, and the coolness with which his revolutionary enthusiasms were received in other countries. This much is no more than a sampling which might be extended throughout the community of nations. Indeed, it is less than a sampling, for it touches upon only a few of the more obvious factors which have combined with others to make the national tradition what it is for each of the nations noted. We are concerned, in truth, with something that is largely imponderable. It may be possible to name or describe or even measure important elements, but about all we can say of the whole is that it is incommensurable and that each has its own.

These factors—polity, culture, and tradition—whether measurable precisely or not, are factors of which account must be taken by those who work with the Law. How otherwise, where ideologies diverge widely, could disagreements on such matters as the judicial function, the individual freedoms, state trading, or private property ever be understood or usefully reconciled? How even a modest beginning with difficult questions of national responsibility for private subversive activities directed against a nation from bases of operation on the territory of another? How deal with minorities, for example, without first knowing what they are and why they present problems? It seems obvious that account must be taken. Nor is international law altogether unique in this respect. It is only more extensively and consistently concerned with these things because of the nature of its community. It is different because it is international.

VII

Such in survey are the elements of which nations are made. Such are the materials of their life and being and the principal factors of forecast with respect to their behavior. Such are the nations, approximately fourscore in number, which together constitute the community of nations.

Among the members of this community there are some attributes or characteristics which are found in each. Each has a homeland, a human population, a governmental structure, and a measure of autonomy, generally well-nigh complete, which custom and circumstance have accorded the national state. Each has with other nations a more or less extensive intercourse which has been conducted generally in conformity with an established practice. Each is a subject of international law, a system of practices and principles found in customs and agreements. At this point, among members of the community, the common characteristics become overlaid increasingly with important dissimilarities of circumstance or condition.

There are smaller groups of nations within the larger community which have more in common than the whole. Thus there are lesser groupings which are characterized in varying degrees by a predominance of common racial stocks or common cultural origins. For some lesser groupings there are also basic similarities of language and for others a common religious faith. We think in this connection of Britain together with certain members of the British Commonwealth and the United States, or of certain of the Latin American republics, or of certain of the Arab nations of the Middle East. There are also lesser groupings which have in common a dependence upon the waterways and resources of the sea, or an excess or deficiency of population in relation to resources, or a similarity of political traditions and ideologies. There are groups having national economies which are predominantly agrarian, and others whose economies are characteristically industrial. Among certain nations international trade is of necessity the dominating feature of the economy, while for others it appears superficially at least to be a factor of less vital importance. Such similarities of interest and outlook within the lesser groupings have a twofold effect: on the one hand, not infrequently, they make understanding easier, particularly among those confronted with similar problems and able to communicate in a common language; on the other hand, they sometimes tend to encourage the formation of interest groups or blocs which bestir jealousies or fears among those situated differently. The net gain or loss in effect upon mutual understanding and accommodation among members of the larger community is not something which can be swept up in broad generalizations. In the long run there is probably a net gain, though much depends upon time and circumstance.

Aside from the identities noted as regards basic attributes of nationhood, and the more restricted and special similarities which have just been instanced, it is apparent that common circumstance is the uncommon thing. Actually the community of nations is a community of vast and pervasive dissimilarities. No two are alike. No two are likely to be conscious of more than a residuum of common interest, and more often than otherwise the residuum will be a thing of varying content. Among members of the community there must always be a common interest in order, but each member's response to the requirements of order will be conditioned by national interest, outlook, and conception of the just principle. It is patent that reconciliation and the subordination of local interests to general law must present tasks of magnitude and unique complexity.

It is patent, indeed, that those who work successfully with law in such relationships must be seasoned in two obvious and compelling conclusions, one of negative import, and the other affirmative in its principal implications. Negatively, they must be on guard at every stage against the perils of oversimplification. It will be convenient and frequently necessary to conceive of nations as entities and subjects of international law; but the neat ascription to them of human attributes, the facile comparison with more homogeneous members of an existing federation, or the divorcement otherwise of lawyers' rationalizations from the actualities of international life can serve only to confuse and frustrate the essentials of useful thinking. So far from contributing anything constructive, they tend to substitute for the devices of a practical jurisprudence the futilities of speculation suspended in space. Affirmatively, the architects, builders, and administrators of a useful international law must be prepared at all times to support their work on firm understandings of the nations with whose problems or relationships they may be concerned. They must be prepared to approach each nation, not primarily as a metaphysical concept, but rather as a body compounded of land, people, economy, and polity, a way of living and a cultural tradition and a veritable complex of hopes, fears, and aspirations. These things may not be by-passed safely as matters outside the law. They are bone, flesh, and life of the law, largely explaining its frustrations and failures in the past and pointing up its prospects for expanded usefulness in the future.

The Law of Nations

I

THE LAW of the community of nations has long been identified by an adjective of doubt with respect to its essential legal nature. It has been "international" in the sense that it has rested basically upon an implied or express acquiescence on the part of the nations in community. Historically it has developed chiefly as custom supplemented by agreement. Possibly it would be more accurate today to describe it as agreement supplemented by custom. In any case its principles and practices have been found in the varied and widely scattered records of international relations. Its scheme or system has been largely the work of publicists or jurists whose researches and writings over the past three or four hundred years have contributed something of form and shape to the amorphous mass. Substance has been a principal determinant of system; and system, in turn, has had more than a little influence upon substance. If we keep well in mind what has been said hitherto with respect to the community of nations, and recall also that up to very recent years this community has been entirely unorganized, we shall be prepared to find in the law of nations a great deal that falls far short of being either comprehensive or adequate. It could hardly be otherwise. Perhaps we shall be most impressed that it has been possible to develop so much that is so useful in such a community.

Certainly we cannot expect to find comprehensive coverage of even the more obvious social needs in a society so loosely knit. Until the social effort has been better organized, there must remain many and important areas which are but partially subject to the rule of law. In these areas shifting political considerations will be found controlling, the ways of international life will be correspondingly rough, and the law will find its principal expression in generalities or postulates but imperfectly implemented as means of accommodation. We find one such area at what should be logically the very threshold of the system.

II

It is said that the subjects of international law are nations, the same variant bodies hitherto considered in our discussion of the international community. They are defined in law as bodies politic or states, of substantial population, occupying fixed territory, under competent government, and having capacity to enter into relationships with other international subjects. Thus conceived, it is noted perforce that nations are born in consolidation, in revolution, secession or separation, or in the determination of a controlling group of powers to establish and recognize a new nation within territory previously belonging to another. Consolidation, revolution, separation, concerted determination and the like are words descriptive of processes which are essentially political. There has been and it is not altogether clear as yet that there can be more than a thin residuum of rule or principle for the governance of such business. Accordingly, the system has largely excluded the birth of the nation as matter of politics rather than of law, and has left us with the conclusion, perforce, that there is no legal right to be born, much less a legal right to be born to any particular condition or status.

Nor is the actual birth of the nation, in a physical sense, necessarily followed by emancipation from politics and subordination to the rule of law. The assurances of normal life and of the privileges of normal intercourse with other nations may come only through political recognition. Other nations must first doff the diplomatic hat. And they must continue to acknowledge as they meet since, as a practical matter, the continuance of orderly relationships is contingent upon continued recognition. Such recognition may be given in a wide variety of ways and it may be granted or denied for an infinity of reasons. It may be express or implicit, joint or several, formal or informal. As a matter of good neighborhood, the timing is frequently important. The thing of note is that the granting, withholding, or withdrawing of recognition, whether in relations with the newborn nation or with the government through which the newborn nation presents itself to the world, is resolved ultimately as a matter of political expediency. There is firmly established neither a right to recognition nor a duty to recognize. In the result, the international system has largely excluded the entire business, restricti its precepts to the import of methods and the consequences of action or inaction.

Born in political readjustment or upheaval, and acknowledged by political recognition in quarters sufficiently influential to give it some assurance of continued life, the nation takes its place in a system of law which accords it important rights and imposes, in imperfect measure, corresponding duties. We shall have more to say presently of the nation's rights, of the imperfection of its duties, and of the reasons therefor which have been characteristic of the international system. Meanwhile we must note that the most important right of all, the right to life, has been in actuality so hedged about with political qualifications as to be almost nonexistent. It is true that the nation's right to life has been asserted frequently, over the years, as a fundamental principle or precept of global jurisprudence. An earthier and somewhat more cautious approach, however, has suggested that the right depends upon the impact of the nation's conduct upon other members of the international society. As one of our most respected publicists has observed, "the welfare of that society may not require the maintenance of a particular state; its very extinction may be deemed to be for the general good." The actualities of practice, indeed, have lent a negligible support to assertion of the more embracing ideal. We recall no instance in history in which the extinction of a nation has been justified in legal conclusions formulated through legal procedures. There have been a good many extinctions and it may be that more would have been warranted, but always they have been the result of political misadventure. Always they have been justified, with at most a thin gloss of juridical apologetics, upon grounds of political expediency. Until ways have been found to make the practices of nations more orderly and humane, the assertion that the nation has a right to life must be regarded as a somewhat academic postulate better known in the breach than the observance.

In brief, there is, or at least there has been in the past, neither right of birth, of recognition, or of continued existence in the international community of law. Broad assertions to the contrary have remained postulates without vitalizing support in actual practice. Thus the system has been obliged to rest its beginnings upon the unstable basis of political opportunism. It has had no choice other than to take the nations as it finds them in any given period. Its precepts and principles have been initiated in rationalization of the community of nations as it exists today; if there are political changes on the morrow, rationalizations may have to be readjusted accordingly. The dominance of politics over law in this important area has remained substantially complete.

In taking the nations as it finds them, with negligible concern for the circumstances of their birth, acknowledgment or life, the system has cultivated a further and extraordinary myopia with respect to all but one of the significant variances which exist among them. It has rationalized each as a corporate body or juridical entity under law and proceeded in cultivated disregard of every difference except the differences in degree of political dependence. The community of nations has thus been presented in law as consisting of independent and dependent states, the former equal in the sense that they resemble each other in enjoying a comparable freedom from outside control in the management of their internal and external affairs, the latter in varying degree subordinate to the control of others. Dependencies are found difficult of satisfactory analysis or useful classification and have been presented generally in rough groupings as mandates, neutralized states, protectorates, suzerainties, unions of states and the like, with liberal reference to the more important historical examples. The hope of independence which so generally characterizes dependent peoples has been passed over lightly and without firm assurance of right to attain the more satisfying status. Like so much else of consequence in international life, both the hope and its realization have remained essentially political matters. Other and more important variances, such as differences in area, location, resource, population, economy, culture, government and the like, are either ignored or dismissed as political variances without juridical import. Thus the law appears to have moved timidly and within a narrowly restricted sphere, leaving most of the things that count to the less refined processes of political adjustment.

Paradoxically enough, within the narrow confines of the little realm which the international system has attempted to make its own, the law has spoken in more strident voice, its confidence fortified by the same political anarchy from which it has recoiled elsewhere. The nation is presented, once its political independence is established, as enjoying a juridical freedom from external control that is significantly embracing. The legal incidents of independent nationhood are said to include the right to acquire and hold territory, to adopt whatever form of government the nation chooses, to enact such laws as it may see fit, to determine the allegiance of its nationals, and generally to treat them as it may see fit, to control the admission of persons into its territory, to expel objectionable persons or classes of persons, to determine freely the kind and amount of intercourse it will have with other nations, to exclude the unwarranted intervention of others in its domestic or foreign affairs, and to resort to force in self-defense. Within the widest of limitations the nation is assertedly free, as matter of legal right, to live its own life in its own way. Its rights are presented characteristically in a bold and embracing system.

The nation's duties, significantly enough, have been presented much more cautiously. In acquiring and holding territory it should respect the rights of others. Its choice of constitution or government is of no concern to the international community unless the form of government adopted is notoriously opposed to the existing international order or calculated to leave the nation incapable of discharging its conceded international obligations. Its right to legislate should not be so exercised as to expose it to a well-founded charge of disregard for international duty. While it may generally do as it pleases with respect to its own nationals, it may be "contemptuous of the dictates of humanity" only at risk of humanitarian protests and perhaps, in the light of recent decisions in the trial of war criminals, at risk of a sterner retribution. While exclusions may be broadly discriminatory, those aimed at areas or races are recognized as a source of profound political resentments; and neither exclusions nor expulsions may be utterly arbitrary or in bad faith. Freedom of intercourse may not be frustrated by retreat into complete isolation. Restraints on intervention are somewhat vaguely conditioned by reference to the intervention's scope and the gravity of the misconduct which is alleged in justification; and resort to force in self-defense may not be a subterfuge for self-aggrandizement.

Thus it is that in matters pertaining to the birth, acknowledgment, life, and liberty of its subjects the international system of law has attempted little more than a rationalization of prevailing political anarchy. Expediency and policy have held extensive areas against the encroachments of right and duty. There has been persistent emphasis upon rights, while correlative duties were left ill-defined, precariously established, or matter of hope. More often than otherwise, the duty to be decent has been discernible only in the formulae of juridical aspiration. Where asserted rights were in conflict the play of self-help has had an embracing significance. Notwithstanding its great age, the system has remained a legal order of impressive immaturity.

III

From the nations as subjects of international law we may pass appropriately, in our survey of the system, to nationals as its most important objects. Surely human population is the nation's most significant feature in its external no less than in its internal relations. How human beings become identified legally as members of the nation body and what the nation may do to them and for them within the ambit of its acknowledged powers and responsibilities are surely matters of paramount importance. Here, again, we find the broadest generalizations of principle, a timidity of principle in its encounters with political actualities and a considerable frustration of practical jurisprudence upon the hard rocks of divergent national interests and conditions.

The system regards nationals as persons who owe allegiance to the nation by virtue of a more or less permanent relationship which the nation determines. They are human beings who have become members, by one criterion or another, of the national body. It is said that the power of the nation to confer such membership is not unlimited; and it would seem obvious that there may be circumstances in which nationality may not be imposed without the acquiescence of the person concerned. The question arises infrequently, however, and in practice the area within which the nation is free to act is wide indeed. The determination of problems of nationality requires a reference to national laws of widely varying provisions.

Nationality is conferred upon a person at birth or by naturalization. Nationality at birth is conferred *jure soli,* by virtue of the place, or *jure sanguinis,* by virtue of blood, or by some combination of the two. From an examination of the nationality laws of some seventy countries made a number of years ago, one of our best informed experts on the subject found that seventeen were based solely upon *jus sanguinis,* two equally upon *jus soli* and *jus sanguinis,* twenty-five principally upon *jus sanguinis* but partly upon *jus soli,* and twenty-six principally upon *jus soli* and partly upon *jus sanguinis.* These tabulations would be somewhat different today, but the essentials would not be changed. It would thus appear that some combination of the two principles is to be found in the laws of most countries, that international law excludes neither and prefers neither, and that both multiple nationality at birth and statelessness are by no means unlikely phenomena.

Nationality by naturalization is collective where territory is transferred together with the allegiance of its inhabitants, or individual where there is compliance with the conditions and procedures which national laws may prescribe for admission to membership in the national community. Individual naturalization, in turn, may be formal, as where the individual renounces allegiance to one country and swears allegiance to another after compliance with the conditions imposed, or informal, as where a wife becomes naturalized by virtue of the naturalization of the husband, or a child by virtue of the naturalization of the parent. Whether and to what extent naturalization in one country operates to expatriate in another have been "burning questions," long extremely troublesome and still largely unresolved. Conflicts of view have stemmed largely from the conflicting interests of nations of emigration and nations of immigration; and the effort to alleviate such conflicts through treaty arrangements has not been conspicuously successful. At the Hague Conference for the Codification of International Law of 1930, an effort to find general bases of agreement "fell among thorns" and little of substance was accomplished.

What the nation may do to its own nationals international law has regarded traditionally as no other nation's business. There has been a reservation of concern where the individual had also another nationality, but otherwise each nation has remained free to oppress, denaturalize, persecute, or even exterminate such persons as were conceded to be its exclusive subjects. It is superfluous to give examples of the oppressions which have characterized man's inhumanity to man over the years or to call the roll of nations, great and small, which have been conspicuous offenders. The right to denationalize has remained unchallenged and denationalizations *en masse* were phenomena of increasing importance in the period between our latest world wars. There have been persecutions so shocking as to provoke humanitarian protests, but vastly more of inhumanity that has gone unprotested. It is no exaggeration to say that the German extermination camps, in all their incredible horror, were a culminating manifestation of the nation's juridical irresponsibility in the treatment or mistreatment of its subjects. Forecast of a limiting principle appeared in certain of the treaties made at the end of the first world war, and more recently there has been affirmation of repentance in principles applied in the trial and conviction of war criminals, in important provisions of the Charter of the United Nations, and in the pending convention on genocide; but the repentance is recent and a firm regeneration remains to be demonstrated. Down to our own time, in brief, international law with respect to national mistreatment of nationals has been a rationalization of complete license.

What the nation may do to the nationals of another has been a different matter. As a correlative of his allegiance it has been assumed generally that the national is entitled to his country's protection abroad as well as at home. The determination to protect and the nature and scope of interposition in his behalf are of course within his government's discretion, but governments do in practice assert an extensive authority to protect their subjects wherever they may be. They insist upon respect for asserted minimum standards of treatment and there has thus been a continuing stream of international controversies with respect to the treatment of individuals in the relation of national to the one and of alien to the other. During the past century there has developed an interesting and significant practice of disposing of such controversies from time to time through arbitration before commissions or tribunals specially constituted for the purpose. There have been many such arbitrations and thousands of awards or decisions have been handed down. Experience with an adjustment process having many of the characteristics of judicial settlement has thus been cumulative and from this experience useful procedures and principles have emerged.

From the practice noted there has evolved, for example, a general opinion that in the absence of special agreement the claimant in whose behalf a nation interposes should have been its national at the time the claim arose and its national continuously thereafter, at least up to the time when the claim was formally presented. The practice indicates, moreover, that a claim will not be countenanced if the claimant is also a national of the respondent nation. Subject to various exceptions, which are none too sharply defined, the claimant is generally required to have been reasonably diligent in the exhaustion of local remedies before his claim may properly become the subject of diplomatic interposition. Damages may be recovered in the claimant's behalf for wrongful injuries attributable directly to abuse of authority or position on the part of officials or agents of the respondent nation. In varying circumstances the decisions recognize minimum standards of administration which may be ignored only at the risk of international responsibility. Damages may also be recovered in the claimant's behalf for wrongful injuries attributable initially to the acts of private individuals where there is delinquency in prevention or negligence in prosecution. The principle has been found applicable in a wide variety of circumstances and notably in cases of injury to the nationals of other countries through mob violence. A more or less comparable principle has found occasional application in cases of injury to the nationals of other countries by unsuccessful insurgents; but this problem is more complicated and there is divergence of view and considerable confusion of thought. Damages for breach of a concession or contract between the national claimant and the government of another country are in a somewhat different category. The mere breach of such a contract is not generally regarded as an international wrong. The instances are numerous, however, in which breach associated with other delinquencies has been found to justify interposition. While practice has not been uniform, claims conventions have not infrequently embraced claims of contractual origin. The so-called Calvo Clause in such concessions or contracts, formulated in terms intended to exclude diplomatic interposition, has been the subject of long standing controversy still unsettled. In the absence of procedures or principles for the relief of insolvent debtor nations, claims on defaulted public bonds are generally the subjects of diplomatic, rather than legal, adjustment. The Hague Convention of 1907 limiting recourse to armed force for the recovery of contract debts had only a limited acceptance among the nations which were thought to be its principal beneficiaries. Efforts to find bases of clarification and agreement on the broader subject at the Conference on Codification at The Hague in 1930 were unsuccessful.

The international system of law in the area thus briefly reviewed has made progress and has encountered frustration. For each nation the nationality of its peoples has remained an internal matter to be determined in accord with assumed political, military, social, or economic needs. The law has been constrained to move in cultivated disregard of such things, however, its basic assumptions remaining permissive rather than harmonizing, and its reconciliations of conflict somewhat less than impressive. The nation's treatment or mistreatment of its own nationals is not yet the subject of an effective international restraint. The nation's mistreatment of the nationals of others, on the other hand, has been the subject of an impressive legal development; but jurisprudence has been characteristically effective where agreement was relatively easy and characteristically hesitant where variant conditions and interests presented more substantial difficulties. On the one hand, nations able to accommodate immigration, of relatively immature economic development, or in need of foreign capital and enterprise have frequently been somewhat less effective than others in the protection of aliens and correspondingly reluctant to concede responsibility for injuries to the nationals of other countries. On the other hand, nations having population, capital or enterprise for export have frequently been somewhat more effective and in any case correspondingly insistent upon higher standards of protection for their nationals abroad. The gap between nations thus characterized has been notable and has not been satisfactorily bridged. The efficacy of the nation's insistence upon the observance of minimum standards by others has generally been in rather obvious proportion to its relative influence and power.

IV

Continuing our survey, we proceed from consideration of the peoples who owe their allegiance to the nation to the lands which constitute their national home. The nation is a body politic having fixed territory with respect to which there is a multiplicity of problems concerning acquisition, transfer, boundaries, privileges of transit and communication, internal authority and external obligation, and the regime of special privilege. There is a considerable body of customary practice with respect to these matters, and the customs of nations have been extensively supplemented by agreements of both special and general import. The subject matter of international law is perhaps more tangible here than elsewhere, the community of interest has been somewhat more apparent, and in the result the legal order has developed more of substance and coherence. The vital variances in area, location, resource, or condition have been as studiously evaded, however, and there has been comparable retreat in the presence of political actualities.

The nation's title to its territory, we learn, may rest initially upon discovery and occupation, accretion or subjugation, or may be acquired from another by cession, relinquishment, prescription, revolution, or annexation. Of these the law of discovery and occupation took shape in the years of colonial expansion and reached maturity in the nineteenth century only to lose most of its practical importance. It has been thought inapplicable in the polar regions, where other practices or agreements appear to be in the making. Accretion, or the gradual addition to coasts and shores through natural processes, has presented no major difficulties and is of distinctly minor importance. Outright subjugation was a source of title characteristic of the period in which wars of conquest were generally approved and the spoils awarded the victor. As mere might came progressively to be regarded as less of a virtue in itself, conquest was generally given cloak of respectability in the formalities of territorial cession, and the consummation of conquest in cession rendered title by subjugation a matter of historical interest chiefly. Thus, as man has completed the discovery of his earth, the emphasis in the law of territory has shifted from initial acquisition to acquisition by transfer.

The transfer of territory by cession, whether coerced or freely negotiated, is generally solemnized in a formal treaty and in practice appears to have been increasingly affected of late by concern for the interests and desires of the inhabitants of the territory transferred. Transfer by relinquishment is infrequent and relatively unimportant. The possibility of transfer by prescription, as by long-continued possession under claim of right, is recognized in the international system; but there is no agreement as to the minimum period of possession, the requirements are left dependent upon the circumstances of the case, and it is generally conceded that occasions for the application of the principle are on the decline. Transfer by revolution is perfected by the revolution's success.

Transfer by annexation may formalize an actual agreement freely negotiated, or an agreement consummated in the presence of superior force, or it may be no more than a name for the *fait accompli* of absorption where resistance would presumably have been futile. In the latter instance, at least, it is scarcely more than subjugation under another name. The more ruthless procedures of an earlier day have a tendency to reappear garbed in the somewhat less offensive terminologies of modern rationalization.

However achieved, whether by cession, revolution, annexation, or otherwise, the transfer of territory from one nation to another presents further problems with respect to the effect of the transfer upon laws in force, private property, contracts and concessions, and the public debt. There is customary practice with respect to these matters, a modicum of agreement, a considerable body of speculative comment, and, on the whole, more of discord than harmony of view. Legislative and political power go with the transfer, of course, but laws for the governance of the general social order continue in effect until they are changed by the nation to which the territory is transferred. It was formerly thought that rights in private property remained unaffected, an assumption rather consistently supported by nineteenth-century practice, but more recent transfers to nations committed to an extensive socialization of property have given rise to an increasing uncertainty of principle. It has been thought that contracts and concessions of local benefit, at least, should be respected by the new sovereign, but here again the signs of an earlier trend have lost something of their former predictive value. In the absence of agreement at the time of transfer, we cannot be sure. As regards the public debt, it is arguable that purely local debts should go with the land, that an apportionment of territory should be accompanied by an equitable apportionment of the general debt, and that transfer of an entire territory should carry with it a general succession to fiscal obligations. The argument encounters no end of political difficulties, however, which are more often evaded than frankly faced, and we may only conclude that there is a host of problems for which the international system of law has yet to find satisfactory solutions.

The nation's boundaries are established at artificial or natural frontiers and have provided the subject matter of both firmer custom and more sharply defined conflicts of interest and view. With improvements in the techniques of cartography, artificial boundaries present fewer difficulties than formerly. The watershed line of boundary hills or mountains is simple in principle and frequently difficult of application. River boundaries generally follow the imaginary midline of the navigable channel or, in streams which are not navigable, a line in the middle of the river. Frontiers in the marginal sea are another matter. Here there is sharp division between those countries which, like the United States, have contended vigorously for a three-mile belt of territorial waters, and other countries which have contended with equal vigor for a wider zone. There is even lack of agreement concerning the manner of drawing a line between territorial waters and the high seas. The most that can be said on this important subject is that nations are generally agreed that their national waters should extend seaward for at least three marine miles. The Hague Conference for the Codification of International Law of 1930 could only report difference of opinion as to the width of the zone, and no attempt was made to submit a convention. As regards national bays there is even less of agreement. Common use of the term "historic bays" is significant. As the term suggests, nations have in fact remained free to decide, within the broadest of limitations, and each for itself, what bays or arms of the adjacent seas are to be regarded as a part of the national domain and dealt with accordingly. There is no simple formula and the Hague Conference was able to establish none. Similarly there are "historic straits" rather than bases of general agreement. In the presence of widely variant conditions of physical geography and political interest, the lawyer's quest for bases of agreement on principles of universal application has hitherto been fruitless and is, in all probability, a misdirected effort.

Within the territory of each nation, other nations have enjoyed in behalf of their nationals important privileges of transit, communication, trade, and travel. It could hardly be otherwise, indeed, if there is to be a community of international life. Such privileges are established by custom or are defined in the more detailed and elaborate provisions of bilateral or multilateral agreements. Thus there is a customary privilege of innocent passage for the ships of one nation in transit through the marginal seas of another. Similarly there is a customary privilege of refuge for ships in distress; and there is also a privilege of access to ports for the commercial vessels of other nations, though each nation reserves an embracing discretion in determining which ports shall be open to commerce and in regulating permissible access. The more important and intricate details of the international system are found chiefly in treaties. The regimes of straits, waterways, and rivers have frequently been established by treaty with advantageous regard for the commercial, geographic, or political interests of the nations concerned. The treaty system for rivers of international importance has had a development that is particularly noteworthy. While there has yet to be acknowledged any general obligation to yield privileges of transit by land, there is here also an important and expanding body of conventional arrangement. Postal communication has long been the subject of a comprehensive system of treaty regulation; and the control of cable and telegraphic communication has had a comparable but somewhat more localized development. Although communication and transport by air are more recent developments, radio is already the subject of an embracing treaty system, and agreements for the governance of air transport are now multiplying rapidly as the need compels. The latter development is still somewhat immature and it is too early to forecast whether the tendency will be toward liberalization of privilege or toward the maintenance of rigid national controls. Perhaps most embracing in their assurances of a mutually beneficial intercourse of communication, travel, and trade have been the innumerable commercial treaties which, in one pattern or another, have long been a characteristic feature of our international relations. Such treaties are a network which literally covers the earth, and their varying provisions are generally in realistic accord with the varying interests and needs of the nations among which they have been concluded. It is odd, but perhaps characteristic, that the juristic systematizers have largely neglected these treaties, presumably because their variances are not easily presented in the generalities of juristic systematization.

Within its territory, except as it has acquiesced in a limiting custom or has expressly agreed to accord privileges to others, the nation's authority is prima facie exclusive and supreme. There is no earthly notion that is higher or more unrestrained than the notion of territorial sovereignty. Thus each nation asserts within its limits an ultimate and final authority with respect to the relations of its inhabitants with one another and with their government, the ownership and control of property, the organization and regulation of pursuits and occupations, the governance of trade and exchange, the enactment and enforcement of the necessary laws, the preservation of order and the administration of justice, and the definition and protection of civil and political liberties. It might be thought, since nations are regarded as themselves the subjects of an international law, that territorial supremacy should beget correlative obligation and that each internal right should be matched in practice by recognition of some sort of external duty. There are germinal indications of such a juridical balance, but more often than otherwise they have been sporadic and have remained imperfectly developed.

The imperfections of duty invite many and characteristic illustrations. We have commented hitherto upon the nation's traditional irresponsibility as regards the treatment of its own nationals. Even as regards its responsibility for the mistreatment of the nationals of others, there has been a hesitant and faltering progress of the law in the presence of sharply diverging conditions and interests. While it has been strongly held in some countries that sovereign control of the ownership and enjoyment of property must be balanced by duty to compensate the nationals of other countries when their property is taken by public authority, the duty has been as strongly repudiated in other lands where property is regarded differently. The conditions of occupation and trade have differed so much in different countries that no more than residual notions of national obligation have been developed. It has been said that the correlative of territorial supremacy is an obligation to maintain justice. However, justice has had a varying content in the understandings of different peoples. So the freedoms considered fundamental in one land have frequently had no effective counterpart in another. Generalities of national duty have been affirmed from time to time, but usually in fragmentary pattern and without firm support in a consistent practice.

The regimes of special privilege for the benefit of one nation in the territory of another are matters of special agreement and are as varied as the circumstances which prompt their establishment. They are in form privileges of occupation and use, as leases, or privileges of exploitation, as of fisheries, mines, or the like, or privileges of passage, as where access to ports or rights of transit are stipulated for an inland country, or privileges of security, where it is agreed that places or frontiers shall remain unfortified and devoted exclusively to pacific use. The system sometimes rationalizes these arrangements of privilege as constituting a legal limitation upon the territorial authority of one nation for the exclusive benefit of another, at other times as a mere matter of bargain and agreement. Where the arrangement is enforced by superior power, as it not infrequently is, there is perhaps something to be said for the rationalization of limited authority. Otherwise the rationalization of agreement is probably to be preferred. A firm pattern of practice is lacking and caution in juridical generalization is undoubtedly the more realistic course.

It would thus appear that the international law of territory and of territorial authority is something of considerable substance. The title to the national domain is understood and firmly established. Transfers of national domain are rationalized in realistic deference to the actualities of national conduct. There is a confusion of practice with respect to the effects of transfer, but publicists have usually been correspondingly cautious in generalization. The law of boundaries is a paradox of accepted principles at some points and of diverging contentions at others. Privileges of transit, communication, trade, and travel rest upon a modicum of accepted custom which has been impressively supplemented in an accumulation of special and general agreements. Though jurists may despair of reducing the accumulation to system, it is nevertheless an indication of what coöperation may accomplish even amidst the anarchy of an unorganized community of widely variant subjects. The *bête noire* of territorial law is of course the unrestrained supremacy of territorial authority. Few limitations are acknowledged, and the development of correlative duty has had no more than a halting and imperfect progress. Within the area assigned to this part of our subject, there is thus both substance and useful systematization. There is also much evasion of the basic factors which make nations behave like nations, much timidity in the presence of geographic, economic, political or other eccentricities, and a tendency to find refuge in postulates which frequently are too embracing to either describe the present or forecast the future.

V

In natural sequence we come now to that part of the international legal system which, although it may sometimes confuse laymen, is preëminently an area of lawyers' delight. We refer to the aggregate of notions and practices described conveniently in a phrase as the "nation's jurisdiction." Literally, the word "jurisdiction" means a speaking in conformity with right, and thus happily describes the authority to govern. The nation has an extensive authority to govern its nationals, wherever they may be, and within its own territorial domain it is primarily and well-nigh exclusively responsible for determining what the law shall be, how the law shall be administered, and the means and methods of its application in the adjustment of controversies. These responsibilities the nation discharges through the legislative, executive, and judicial arms of its government. If there were few overlappings or conflicts of jurisdiction among nations, limitations of authority would be correspondingly unimportant and it would perhaps be enough to say that, within its proper sphere and the bounds of decency, each nation may govern as it pleases. Actually, of course, there is a vast amount of overlapping and conflict and the development of corresponding adjustments and limitations has long since been recognized as a prime necessity of international intercourse.

The modern nation ordinarily has a considerable force

of persons and things assigned, in the classical definition of a diplomat, to "lie abroad" in the service of the country. Thus, at the threshold of relations between nations the public authority of one overlaps or is in conflict with the public authority of another. No nation may subject another to its jurisdiction without the latter's consent. The visiting chief of a foreign government is accorded local exemptions for himself and his entourage. Comparable immunities now protect the officials who represent nations at international organizations. Indeed, international organizations as such are by agreement generally exempted from the exercise of local authority. Over the years, in deference to the familiar sensitivities of sovereigns and as an aid to orderly intercourse, there has developed an embracing scheme of jurisdictional immunities or exemptions which cover both the agents and the instrumentalities of modern international relations. In the case of diplomatic personnel, the immunities are firmly founded on ancient custom, fortified and defined in a substantial body of national laws and decisions and, except as regards the exemptions which may be claimed in behalf of the unofficial staff, are the subject of a substantially uniform practice. Historically, consular officials were not diplomatic officers and could not claim the same immunities as of right. Under modern consular conventions, however, they are accorded a wide variety of privileges and immunities considered essential to their successful functioning. The foreign military force entering a nation with its consent or, if the expedition is internationally justified or excusable, without its consent, is almost completely exempt from any local authority. Substantially similar is the position of a visiting foreign warship or ship devoted to foreign public service. The increasing nationalization of merchant vessels and their employment in commercial enterprise under government controls have raised more difficult questions with respect to which practice is divergent or unsettled. Comparable problems are in the making with respect to foreign state aircraft; and uncertainties arising from the increasing tendency of nations to acquire and use property abroad have been thought to require further agreement if international law is to remain flexibly responsive to modern needs.

The modern nation is solely responsible for its own regime of public order. Accordingly it has an unquestioned jurisdiction to define and punish crime in conformity with its own traditions and through its own laws and public authorities. A generality of principle is not difficult to formulate, but actual allocation of authority among neat national compartments encounters at once an infinity of complications. Thus it is recognized everywhere that the nation may define and punish crimes committed within its territory; but the so-called territorial principle has been so extended in modern practice, whether through laws expanding the definition of particular crimes, or through laws extending the scope of the territorial concept, that an initial simplicity of principle is soon lost in the maze of its practical applications. There are similar complications with respect to crimes committed on the nation's public or private ships and presumably with respect to crimes committed on its aircraft wherever they may be. Outside the national domain or places assimilated thereto, the nation has jurisdiction with respect to any crime committed anywhere by one of its nationals and probably, to a limited extent at least, by persons assimilated to nationals. Most nations assert a more or less comprehensive jurisdiction with respect to crimes committed by aliens outside the territory against the safety of the state. A considerable number of nations also assert jurisdiction of crimes against nationals, wherever committed, as well as a jurisdiction which is universal in theory but generally circumscribed by practical safeguards. In the result there is a vast deal of overlapping and a corresponding need for the reconciliation of conflicts.

The increasing facility of communication and travel in modern times has long since compelled an increasing coöperation among nations in the mutual surrender of fugitives from criminal justice. There is no obligation to surrender apart from treaty; but actually, during the past one hundred and fifty years, the world has come to be increasingly encompassed by a network of extradition agreements. The scope of these agreements has been progressively extended, moreover, and the procedures improved. There are indications, indeed, that considerable groups of nations have now reached the point at which it may be considered practicable to supersede a multiplicity of bilateral treaties with multilateral treaties of extradition of general rule-making effect. Notwithstanding the difficulties which have been encountered with respect to such problems as the surrender of nationals, the definition of nonextraditable political offenses, and the interpretation of particular treaty provisions, the growth of an international treaty law of extradition has provided hopeful evidence of the capacity of nations to coöperate effectively where there is a substantial common interest and where the need for coöperation is sufficiently appreciated.

The modern nation is likewise responsible for its own regime of private right and duty; and here, in a body of principle and practice locally called the Conflict of Laws and elsewhere more commonly described in congenial phrase as Private International Law, the nations have learned to adjust the conflicts and overlappings of their authority upon a live and let-live basis. There is a host of problems concerning the adjudication and regulation of matters of private right and duty which arise uniquely from the continuing movement of persons or things from one nation to another and from the increasing ease with which relationships of agreement, family, property, enterprise, or the like may be consummated across national frontiers. Life on this planet refuses to be segregated by national boundaries. When and in what circumstances may the nation's courts hear and decide disputes involving alien visitors or its own or alien subjects *in absentia?* What recognition and effect will the courts of one country accord to adjudications of the courts of another? In what law will the courts of a nation find the appropriate rule of decision when the facets of a controversy are in one way or another identified with several lands? These and a multiplicity of related questions of private law have been the subject of an evolving jurisprudence having important international ramifications. Here judges and jurists have proceeded, largely without benefit of diplomatic interposition or foreign office concern, in the development of a law having world-wide import. More recently, particularly during the past fifty years, there has been a notable effort to achieve more of unification through general international treaties. Though retarded and confined by traditional divergences of view between nations of the Roman Civil Law, on the one hand, and nations of the English Common Law, on the other, the effort has had a considerable success. There are not only groups of nations among which a substantial unification has been achieved, but contained also in the movement are chart and forecast of useful things to come.

Overlappings of authority and corresponding problems of adjustment are the rule rather than the exception in important areas of maritime jurisdiction. In general ships on the high seas are subject exclusively to the authority of the nation whose flag they fly. When merchant vessels flying the flag of one nation put into the ports of another, it might be assumed that they would pass wholly under the jurisdiction of the latter and there is much theoretical assertion to that effect. Practically, however, it has been found convenient to recognize limitations on the jurisdiction of the territorial sovereign with respect to internal matters affecting the ship and its occupants only. Whether such limitations rest upon comity, or upon a binding custom, or upon the provisions of treaties has been disputed. Whatever the approved theory, the practice is general. If the foreign ship is forced into port in distress it is conceded an even larger measure of exemption under customary law. Likewise if it is passing through the marginal seas in innocent passage. It is with respect to the high seas outside the maritime belt, and particularly with respect to the adjacent seas where problems of protective jurisdiction are acute, that practice has remained less settled and jurists have been less successful in their endeavors to rationalize the authority which nations actually assert. The foreign ship which offends within territorial waters and flees to the high seas may be taken thereon in a "hot pursuit" commenced in territorial waters. Presumably the foreign ship which offends within territorial waters from a position immediately outside or adjacent thereto may be taken on the high seas, as a protective measure, if the nation whose flag the ship flies is unable or unwilling to prevent or abate the wrong. Over foreign vessels inbound most maritime nations exercise a more or less extensive protective jurisdiction outside the maritime frontier in the enforcement of their revenue, sanitary, sumptuary, police, or security laws. While the validity of the general principle must undoubtedly be admitted, the scope of its permissible application is anything but clear and important maritime nations are prone to assert against others assumed limitations which their own conduct has belied. As regards hovering ships under foreign flag, there is confusion of practice and even less of clarifying rationalization. On the high seas as such, and aside from the jurisdiction over national ships and the protective jurisdiction over foreign ships which has just been noted, there is firm customary authority only with respect to pirates and a closely restricted treaty authority in conventions for the suppression of the slave trade, the traffic in arms, or pelagic sealing.

In or under the high seas are vast riches of marine life and mineral resource which may be of immeasurable benefit to mankind if properly conserved. It is unfortunate that jurisdiction to conserve has been largely frustrated in times past by familiar negations. Suggestively entitled "the exploitation of the riches of the sea," the subject has been presented generally as requiring a measure of cooperation among nations which was difficult or impossible of achievement at the time. In the result, except for the "special equities" which certain nations have asserted successfully in banks or sedentary fisheries near their coasts and the special regimes which have been established by treaty among such nations as were willing to coöperate in regulating sealing, whaling, or certain types of deep sea fishing, the conservation of sedentary, deep sea, or anadromous marine life has remained largely a matter of hope. As means of exploiting have been developed, similar frustrations have threatened to impede the conservation of mineral and other resources in the soil under the sea. Here quite recent developments are significant. Following initiative taken by the United States in 1945, a number of countries have asserted jurisdiction over the natural resources of their contiguous sea bed in the interest of conservation and prudent utilization. The limits of the jurisdiction asserted have been set at the edge of the continental shelf, at an arbitrary depth, or at an arbitrary distance, depending upon the local physiography. National action thus appears to have produced results where international coöperation was formerly frustrated. There will be new conflicts to reconcile, of course, and it is possible that ultimately a more effective international coöperation may be stimulated.

Without probing further into the intricacies of jurisdictional conflict and reconciliation in international life, it will perhaps be enough to say that the subject presents some of the international system's more substantial achievements. No doubt this is to be attributed to the circumstance that the subject embraces many sources of conflict and irritation but few of the great prizes for which nations fight. An increasing multiplicity of contacts in the less explosive areas of international relations has encouraged a progressive development of the techniques and principles of accommodation. Here national legislation has frequently followed a pattern suggested by international custom, and here it has been notably possible for national courts to make distinctive contributions through their decisions in cases of international import. Here somewhat more than elsewhere customs of general acceptance and practical utility have slowly emerged. The supplementing of custom through agreements of rule-making effect has been substantial.

As must have been anticipated, there are also subjects of unsettlement or tardiness of agreement which are no less notable. Earlier differences among national political systems have given way to new divergences of social and economic purpose and the nation in commerce has presented new problems which are not easily resolved through the application of old principles and procedures. There are conflicts of public jurisdiction in penal matters which continue to be exaggerated, in part naturally because of variances of culture and administration, and in part needlessly in reliance upon unwarranted generalizations from superficial analyses of practice. There are also conflicts of jurisdiction in matters of private right and duty which persist, in part, because of divergences of legal tradition, but rather more, it would seem, because of timidity of approach to the problems of reconciliation. The adjustment of conflicts of jurisdiction upon the sea, notwithstanding its increasing importance, has left much that is unresolved, while principles to govern the conservation and prudent utilization of resources in or under the sea have emerged only recently from the planning stage. Within the broader areas of the nation's jurisdiction there are firm bases upon which to build. Experience had with the methods and techniques of accommodation has been especially valuable. There remains also much building to be done.

VI

In a world as interdependent as the one in which we live, the nation's ultimate service to the human beings who inhabit its lands is manifested in the conduct of international relationships. Here, generally, we discover the ultimate criteria of its success or failure. Here we find practices of ancient lineage and of a relatively comprehensive development. International law stems, in truth, from the interrelationships of the earliest political groups of the human race. From earliest historic times the groups of man have been concerned in varying degree with the amenities of their inter-group communications and understandings. In our own time, and among members of the modern community of nations, these amenities have come to be largely governed by the law of intercourse and agreement.

At the diplomatic or political level, practices with respect to intercourse are grounded largely upon custom, and embrace among other things the methods and procedures of intergovernmental communication and negotiation, the classification, rank, and precedence of diplomatic representatives, the beginning and end of diplomatic mission, the rights and duties of diplomats, including their jurisdictional immunities, the formalities and techniques of diplomatic negotiation, and various matters of ceremonial. At the commercial or economic level, such practices are defined largely in treaties and embrace the classes of consular officers, their designation and reception, and the varied privileges and immunities which have been found necessary to the discharge of their functions under modern conditions of international life.

Agreements among nations are a necessary incident of their intercourse and it has been noted that they increase in number and variety as intercourse expands and produces "a consciousness of mutual dependency." Measured by the many thousands of treaties and less formal agreements which have been concluded in modern times, it would appear that "a consciousness of mutual dependency" has grown apace. At the same time there has developed a body of practice with respect to agreements, extensively rationalized by resort to private law analogies, concerning the capacity to enter into agreements, the validity of agreements, the requirement of mutual assent, formalities of negotiation and conclusion, effect and observance, interpretation and termination.

Except in the case of dependent nations, capacity to enter into agreements with other nations is assumed to be virtually unlimited. In theory there may be restrictions upon validity, but in practice such restrictions are almost nonexistent. There are no required forms, though agreements falling into conventional categories of greater dignity or permanence are usually expressed in formal treaties or conventions, bilateral or multilateral, while undertakings of more restricted or less enduring import may find expression in a *modus vivendi,* a protocol, an executive agreement, or the like. The requirement of public registration was first formulated in the League of Nations Covenant, and has been revised and reaffirmed more recently in the United Nations Charter. Mutual assent must be appropriately and sufficiently manifested, but here there has been striking departure from the most elemental principles of civilized jurisprudence. Assent coerced by force or threat of force, if formally sufficient, has been considered as binding as assent given freely. In the negotiation and conclusion of the more formal agreements, there is commonly observed an impressive and important body of ritual with respect to the authority to negotiate and sign, the formalities of language, the description of parties, the order of signing, the protocols of meetings and signature, and the procedures of ratification, exchange and deposit of ratifications, reservation, and adherence.

Treaties are binding, of course, only upon the parties to the agreement. They may or may not require national implementing legislation, depending upon their terms and the requirements of national law. In the United States the immediate efficacy of treaties requiring no implementing legislation is fortified by a provision of the national Constitution that "all treaties made, or which shall be made, under the authority of the United States, shall be the supreme law of the land; and the judges in every state shall be bound thereby, anything in the constitution or laws of any state to the contrary notwithstanding." There are a few other nations having constitutional provisions of similar effect. *Pacta sunt servanda* is thus translated from the formulae of international jurisprudence into a working precept of national law. Upon the whole, if engagements coerced by force or threat of force are excepted, it will be found that international agreements are as well or even better observed than contracts in private law.

The interpretation of treaties has been the subject of an extensive consideration in both national and international judicial decisions. As in the interpretation of private contracts, the problem is essentially one of ascertaining the sense in which the parties have employed the terms of their choice. The use of different languages has presented special problems; but restrictive rules of evidence, so troublesome in our own common law, have been largely avoided. Real conflicts between plain meaning and the import of extrinsic evidence have been relatively infrequent. The Permanent Court of International Justice made some of its most useful contributions to international law in this field and appears to have been progressively inclined toward discovery of the essential sense of the agreement through realistic resort to all relevant sources of interpretation. The principle of liberal construction, so often affirmed in opinions of the United States Supreme Court, would appear to be chiefly significant as an indication of similar approach. The artificial canons of interpretation which are to be found in some of the treatises on international law have proved of doubtful utility and have been relatively little used.

The termination or suspension of treaties is a subject which has been much mooted over the years and which embraces some major unsettled problems. Naturally a termination in accord with the express terms of the agreement gives rise to few difficulties. The same may be said of the termination of bilateral agreements by subsequent agreement between the two parties. There is more difficulty, for obvious reasons, in the termination of multilateral agreements by subsequent agreement between the parties. Termination or suspension upon the initiative of a single party, whether of bilateral or multilateral agreements and without subsequent agreement among the parties, is sometimes sought to be justified on the ground of changed conditions beyond the contemplation of the parties when the original agreement was made. The one certainty in life is the certainty of change, and it seems clear enough, so long as agreements are made improvidently without provision for their termination or suspension, or are imposed by force upon nations later permitted to recover power, that there must be an implicit reservation of right to terminate as obsolescent, or suspend as inapplicable, in the event that the agreement becomes truly inapplicable through change of circumstance. The practice has been confused and uncertain and there has been a good deal of doctrinaire evasion among the writers. Satisfactory solutions must depend, it would appear, upon an improved organization of the processes of international coöperation and adjudication. Meanwhile, the issue will arise from time to time and will continue to bedevil the good understanding of nations. A change in the form of government of a contracting nation does not terminate its treaties. It is generally otherwise where the identity of the nation itself is wholly lost, but the question of succession to treaty obligations upon a succession of nations or a transfer of territory is a subject of neither clearness of thought nor uniformity of action. Denunciation by one nation because of alleged violations on the part of another has been almost as troublesome as termination or suspension because of changed conditions, and fundamentally for similar reasons. The effect of war upon treaties, whether to abrogate, suspend, or bring into operation, has been extensively considered in theory and practice, and in more recent times has frequently been the subject of appropriate arrangements in the treaty of peace.

In the international law of intercourse and agreement, in summary, we find at once a more impressive indication of the system's antiquity and what is perhaps the stronger evidence of a coherent development. Here there is, upon the whole, rather less of retreat from reality, though here as elsewhere, there is a good deal of legalistic postulating which has at best a tenuous relationship to the actualities of life. In the result there is perhaps no aspect of the system in which its extraordinary paradoxes are so sharply exposed. There is great age and a shocking artlessness. There is much that serves the ends of an ordered justice and much of excessive formalism. As under other legal systems, social adjustment is accomplished largely through continuing discussion and negotiation conducted with substantial respect for accepted standards, but under no other system is there so much concern for the procedures of proceeding or so significant a reliance upon the *vade mecum* of negotiating practice. There is maturity, as in the interpretation of treaties, and retarded development, as in succession to treaty obligations or terminations for breach. There are strong bases of order, as in treaty observance, and recurring invitations to anarchy, as in the reconsideration of inapplicable treaties and in treaties imposed by force. Nowhere, except in the adjustment of international differences, a topic presently to be considered, does emergence from the immature and the inadequate await more obviously upon improved organization of the processes of international accommodation.

VII

Institutions and procedures for the adjustment of differences under law are at once the hope and the despair of all who reflect seriously upon the relations of nations. Law is not in itself a self-propelled vehicle of order. With whatever approach to perfection its standards, principles, and rules may be elaborated in the system of any community, there are bound to be differences and disputes with respect to its application and effect in an infinity of cases. In brief, the law itself is a source of unending controversy. Properly channeled, such controversy is constructive and a contribution to good order. Unchanneled, it may end in fortifying recrimination and strife. The channeling must be achieved, of course, through general acceptance of and confidence in a comprehensive system of adjustment institutions and procedures. In this essential aspect of its progress, the international system of law has been woefully deficient.

As previously suggested, most adjustments of controversy among members of the international community are accomplished, as in any other community, through the continuing processes of discussion and negotiation. Somewhat like the counsellor at law, it is the continuing business of the foreign service official to prevent misunderstanding, allay irritation, and discover bases of compromise and agreement. As previously suggested, also, nations maintain more or less elaborate and costly foreign services to these ends and the international system incorporates a detailed and somewhat formal practice with respect to their functioning. It is when we come to consider the alternative procedures to which recourse may be had when negotiation fails that the deficiencies of the international system become disturbingly apparent. The traditional presentation of alternative procedures is in two grand divisions, viz., amicable modes of adjustment and non-amicable modes short of war. The former include good offices and mediation, commissions of inquiry, commissions of conciliation, arbitration and judicial settlement. The latter are variously described as retorsion, retaliation, reprisal, rupture of diplomatic relations, embargo, non-intercourse, pacific blockade, and the like. The former, down to very recent times, have had a dwarfed and rudimentary development. The latter are obviously mere variations of self-help and more than likely to provide a prelude to violence.

Of the amicable procedures, those of good offices and mediation have been formalized in multilateral treaties but have been used with relative infrequency. Commissions of inquiry and commissions of conciliation have been contemplated or detailed in a great number of treaties, bilateral or multilateral, but upon the whole their use has been negligible. Recourse to arbitration, on the other hand, has had a vastly more impressive and encouraging development. The procedures have been outlined in a great number of treaties, bilateral or multilateral, and have been extensively and successfully used. In the accumulated awards and decisions there is discernible an emerging body of rudimentary principles with respect to the necessary procedural techniques, the competence of tribunals, the interpretation of international instruments, the finality of awards, the disposition of awards in excess of the terms of submission, unconscionable awards, the determination of damages, and kindred matters which should some day contribute substance and efficacy to the legal system. The development has been most impressive, as previously noted, in the settlement of disputes with respect to the alleged mistreatment by one nation of the nationals of another. Its shortcomings are as sharply portrayed in the same phase of the adjustment drama. The tribunals are impermanent, are set up from time to time as disputes accumulate in numbers sufficient to compel the attention of governments, are given a scope of authority determined largely by the expediencies of the moment, and operate under procedures which remain cumbersome and primitive. So far as the unfortunate nationals are concerned, the awards are rarely timely or efficacious but, like the sins of the fathers, are visited upon the children even unto the third and the fourth generations. Too often their bounty is beneficial only to remote kin and to claims attorneys who specialize in such business. The same shortcomings have retarded the use and growth of arbitration in other and broader fields. The cases, great and small, are in addition an impressive multitude, but the patterns of a truly well-ordered progress are not yet discernible. The so-called Permanent Court of Arbitration, organized pursuant to the Hague Conventions of 1899 and 1907 for the Pacific Settlement of International Disputes, has actually been no more than a small administrative office, a panel of available arbitrators and an outline of agreed procedures. Throughout its years it has been used in approximately a score of cases, of which only a few may be said to have been of first-rate importance or to have contributed substantially to the progress of the law.

Judicial settlement in the international sphere is not different from arbitration in its essential features. Each envisages an adjustment in accordance with the law and practice of nations. Unlike the more casual processes of arbitration, however, judicial settlement is assumed to require permanent tribunals and to assure a larger measure of jurisdictional and procedural consistency. It should also assure a somewhat more favorable climate for the progress of the law from precedent to precedent. It had a brief but hopeful history in the Permanent Court of International Justice which was established at The Hague in 1922 as a constituent part of the plan of organized coöperation envisaged in the Covenant of the League of Nations. The Court's life was too brief to give reliable indication of its ultimate significance. In constitution, organization, and procedure it was a truly judicial body. Time and circumstance considered, it had a fair amount of judicial business. While its remoteness from the unsettlements of a disordered world and its relative inaccessibility rendered it chiefly of symbolic importance, in the period in which it served, its contributions to law, particularly in the field of procedure and in the interpretation of international agreements, were an augury of useful service.

The deficiencies of the institutions and procedures of international adjustment under law become all too evident when we take note, as we must, of the overweening importance of self-help as a solvent of international differences. Wherever the assurances of justice according to law are insufficient, there is bound to be in practice a well-stocked store of serve-yourself devices which are neither amicable nor orderly. This is conspicuously illustrated in the international system. There has been and there still is a broad and undefined area within which recourse to such devices is recognized as clearly permissible. Thus retorsion, retaliation, and reprisal have had their place in the practices of nations and have been rationalized and presented with varying refinements of definition. The rupture of diplomatic relations has never been internationally illegal. The embargo has taken various forms and has been pacific or hostile. Non-intercourse has remained a permissible recourse of the nation which would save itself or its nationals from the allegedly illegal or reprehensible conduct of another. Pacific blockade has been a form of blockade having impact presumably only upon the nations immediately concerned, though maritime nations have never been able to agree upon its scope. Such devices, theoretically available to all, have actually been the remedy of the strong against the weak. They will be found to persist in any system in proportion as orderly procedures under law are deficient or lacking. Their mere inclusion in the system of international adjustment is proof beyond refutation that the system is primitive. Placed alongside the procedures of order and decency, they are a continuing invitation to relapse into the law of the jungle. Among nations of comparable resource and power, at least, such relapse is all too likely to be part of the prelude to war.

In the older books of international law, even war was sometimes presented as the ultimate and definitive method of non-amicable adjustment. It was accepted as a more dramatic, though less refined, form of permissible self-help, to be prosecuted according to law and having a host of legal incidents and consequences. Not infrequently the so-called law of war was the subject of a more detailed and systematic presentation on the part of the treatise writer than the law of peace. Its customs, to be sure, embodied a practice of ancient lineage and embracing import. Its humane objectives were the conservation of as much tolerance as could be reconciled with the intolerance of mutual destruction, as much amelioration as could be saved amidst bitterness and hate, and as much order as could be preserved in disorder. Without belittling the importance of such practice in its time and place, it is evident that it has presented at all times the supreme paradox of jurisprudence. It has been law in a restricted and special sense only, for right struggling even feebly against might in a milieu of violence is necessarily a miscast figure of speech. With the transition to total warfare, through modern industrialization and science, there are not many of the older amenities which have been able to survive. There are a few, as the judgments at Nuremberg, Tokyo, and elsewhere have affirmed, but they are no part of a system of remedial adjustment. War in our time has become revolt against an existing condition. It betokens the failure of alternative and insufficient procedures. It is the negation of justice under law.

Thus despair and hope have marched abreast where hope sufficiently implemented must some day point the way to an approaching maturity. Needless to say there has been no such approach to maturity in our time. The long struggle for a minimum of order and decency in the accommodation of international differences has yet to be won. Of amicable modes, only negotiation has come of age; and negotiation unsupported by an informed opinion and the will to understanding is repeatedly frustrated. More pretentious procedures have multiplied on paper but have been little used. There have been glimpses of a firmer order in the long experience with arbitration and the briefer history of judicial settlement, but always they have been caught unsteadily across the desolate no-man's land of self-help, a land strewn with the wreckage of non-amicable adjustment and periodically desolated by war. This is only another way of saying that as regards its institutions and procedures of adjustment the law of nations has been a jungle law imperfectly ameliorated by a fragmentary and hesitant progress in the direction of legal order.

VIII

In this survey of a system we have endeavored to be critical without becoming captious. Within limitations of time and space we have been able to reconnoiter six grand aspects or divisions of the subject. Within each it has been thought that characteristic weaknesses or defects were revealed. It will perhaps be useful at this point to bring together in tentative summary the principal deficiencies which the survey is thought to have disclosed.

Looking first at the nation as the traditional and principal subject of law in the international system, and with attention to its birth, recognition, life, and death, we have been impressed by the exclusion of law from some very important areas of international relationship. Here are vital areas which remain dominated almost exclusively by the unregulated interplay of political forces. Continuing with nationality and the principles which determine human allegiance to the nation, including the severance of allegiance and the protection of nationals abroad, we have taken note perforce of the law's evasions and retreats in the presence of strongly rooted national divergences. Here are important gaps which remain unbridged or spanned with nothing more substantial than unimplemented generalities. The law of the national domain or homeland, including such earthy business as acquisitions, transfers, boundaries, internal authority and external responsibility, has been impressive in its scope and substance and also in its characteristic exaltation of territorial sovereignty. In the unorganized associations of sovereign nations, their national sovereignty has been a dread and fearful thing. The law of jurisdiction has been found to have achieved much, to have developed invaluable techniques of reconciliation, and also to have its lacunae and its exaggerations of sovereignty. Here differences are permitted to persist for one reason or another, notably between countries of the Common Law and countries of the Civil Law, which have long since become differences of description largely rather than differences of substance. It has required no exhaustive survey of the law of intercourse and agreements to reveal extraordinary paradoxes—age and artlessness, maturity and retarded development, order and anarchy—calling urgently for improved organization of the processes of accommodation. Perhaps nothing points up the paradoxes more sharply than respect for the obligations of treaties and treaties made under duress. Finally, in the law and practice which is concerned primarily with the settlement of disputes, there has been apparent on every hand a weakness in the orderly procedures and a corresponding vitality in self-help. The classical dichotomy between "amicable modes" and "non-amicable modes short of war" is the system's most striking self-indictment in this grand division of its subject matter.

The preceding summary will perhaps suggest that the deficiencies observed in various divisions of the law of nations are no more than varying aspects of the same thing. The law has developed among the members of an unorganized community of basically dissimilar subjects. There have been strong traditions of resistance to anything approaching effective organization. Are not subservience to politics, evasions of reality, exaltation of sovereignty, and all the rest such identifying characteristics as we should expect to find in a community so constituted? We may return to this question later. Meanwhile, in the essay to follow, we shall look at the means of growth which are present and at work within the existing system.

The Growth of the Law

I

THERE WERE publicists of an earlier period who were wont to regard the society of nations as a natural society and nations as living in a state of nature. They were not far wrong. In the same vein of thought they were prone to describe much of the law of nations as a natural law made applicable to the relations of nations. Again, if we have succeeded in recapturing something of the meaning which terms had in this earlier writing, it would seem that they were expressing a plausible conviction. When so much of useful and enduring law could be developed by acquiescence or agreement among bodies so separate and dissimilar, it would seem that there must have been at least latent in people a strong natural urge toward order. In this sense, at least, there was something natural about the early law of nations.

The early law of nations was tough law and was perhaps well adapted to slow development in keeping with the requirements of a slowly moving society. As the interdependence of nations increased, however, and as the rudimentary organization of the whole or most of their community began to take shape and the pace of change to accelerate, the conscious extension and improvement of international law became a matter of increasing urgency.

There has been much governmental effort to this end during the past half century. Law without growth is deadwood. Deficient law without means or hope of repairing the deficiencies would appear to be something of singular futility. So it becomes pertinent at this point to inquire concerning the means of growth or the facilities of repair which are to be found within the patterns of the existing system. Where shall we look, in this swiftly changing season, for the signs of a more serviceable development? It should be helpful to relate our answers, for whatever they may be worth, to the shortcomings of international law which were noted in the preceding essay.

II

In the preceding essay we pointed to practices concerning the birth, recognition, life, and death of a nation to illustrate the defect of unregulated vital areas left largely to the interplay of political forces. This shortcoming—the word is here uniquely apt—and also the means of its repair, have been well presented recently in circumstances attending the birth and recognition of the new nation of Israel.

It will be recalled that what is now the Israel homeland was included in a British mandate after the first World War and that after the second World War Britain announced its intention to terminate the mandate. The accumulated problems were debated at length in the Assembly of the United Nations and in November of 1947 a resolution was voted recommending a Plan of Partition and calling upon the inhabitants to take the necessary steps. On May 14, 1948, a provisional government in

Palestine proclaimed the establishment of the state of Israel. On the same day the United States recognized the provisional government as the *de facto* authority of the new state. Recognition on the part of the Soviet Union followed three days later. Among the Arab peoples, hostile to the recognition of a Jewish nation in their midst, there were sinister stirrings.

In the Security Council of the United Nations on May 18, 1948, the representative of Syria criticized the recognition which the United States had been in such haste to accord Israel as precipitate and improper, and suggested that the question be referred to the International Court of Justice. To this the representative of the United States, Mr. Austin, replied: "I should regard it as highly improper for me to admit that any country on earth can question the sovereignty of the United States of America in the exercise of that high political act of recognition of the *de facto* status of a State. Moreover, I would not admit here, by implication or by direct answer, that there exists a tribunal of justice or of any other kind, anywhere, that can pass judgment upon the legality or the validity of that act of my country. There were certain powers and certain rights of a sovereign State which were not yielded by any of the Members who signed the United Nations Charter and in particular this power to recognize the *de facto* authority of a provisional government was not yielded. When it was exercised by my Government, it was done as a practical step, in recognition of realities: the existence of things, and the recognition of a change that had actually taken place. I am certain that no nation on earth has any right to question that, or to lay down a proposition that a certain length of time of the exercise of *de facto* authority must elapse before that authority can be recognized."

These were strong words from the representative of the United States, though it is hardly to be doubted that they depicted with substantial accuracy the anarchy which has prevailed hitherto in such no-law areas as those concerned with birth and recognition. Probably Mr. Austin was substantially correct also in what he said of the sovereign powers which were not intended to be yielded in accepting the United Nations Charter. At the same time, however, he was a leading participant in a process which had been reorganized and reëstablished in the United Nations Charter and which has within it such possibilities of growth as may ultimately make most of what he said appear quaintly irrelevant. When matters of this sort are removed from the realm of separate and uncoördinated political action to become the subjects of study and report, perhaps of debate and vote, in the organs of permanently organized coöperation, there are at least the beginnings of a move from anarchy toward order. We may observe something of this in the subsequent course of events with respect to Israel. Within the year following the proclamation of nationhood, fifty-five governments extended recognition, seventeen *de facto* and thirty-eight *de jure*. Of these, forty-five were members of the United Nations. On May 11, 1949, Israel was admitted by a vote of 37 to 12, with 9 abstentions, as the fifty-ninth member of the United Nations.

As United Nations membership becomes more embracing and as methods are tested and improved, it is entirely possible that the anarchic consequences of separate political action may be subordinated progressively to coordinated and orderly procedures in conformity with such principles as experience has developed. Experience in the areas discussed is at hand or in prospect as regards Indonesia and other new nations of Asia or Africa. Similar problems arising from revolutionary changes of government in older nations may invite similar solutions. This is not to forecast an easy or immediate transition from the discord of sovereignties to the harmony of tested constitutional procedures. No doubt the way will be hard and long. It is only to emphasize that there are means of growth within the existing system. New practices may be germinal, but they are there. It is not inventiveness that is required so much as understanding and persistence.

III

Another deficiency which is much too characteristic is the persistence at many places in the law of important gaps or lacunae. In areas generally covered by a useful legal development there may appear, frequently at the point where controversy becomes most acute, a no-law area of which one may say with assurance only that there is a marked divergence of national interest and corresponding contrariety of opinion. Sometimes the law, like the wandering minstrel, becomes literally a thing of shreds and patches.

Our instances were drawn in the preceding essay from the law of nationality, including expatriation and the protection of nationals abroad. They could have been drawn as well from almost any other grand division of the subject. It appears that such gaps or lacunae persist generally for either of two reasons or for some combination of the two: either the administrators or the makers of the law have chosen deliberately to ignore such disparate factual bases as geography, resource, population, economy, or culture may present, thus foreclosing all possibility of an enduring reconciliation, or there is a timidity of approach to problems deriving from disparate factual bases which amounts to the acceptance of gaps as something present and irremediable among members of the community of nations. In either case the frustration is complete. Neither sort of surrender is necessary. This may be demonstrated by contrasting selected failures and successes in the field of arbitral decision and also in the field of law-making by agreement.

In the field of arbitral decision, we may take as an example of failure that part of the award in the famous North Atlantic Coast Fisheries Arbitration of 1910, between Great Britain and the United States, which dealt with the problem of "bays." A treaty of 1818 had reserved to inhabitants of the United States forever the liberty to take fish within certain limits off the Atlantic coasts of British North America. Outside the agreed limits the United States had renounced any privileges theretofore enjoyed or claimed "within three marine miles of any of the coasts, bays, creeks, or harbors." From where must be measured the three marine miles from any "bays"? There had been many and grievous disputes. The question concerning "bays" was one of seven submitted to an arbitral tribunal of great distinction constituted from the panel of the Permanent Court of Arbitration.

Before the tribunal Great Britain contended generally that the renunciation applied to "bays" in a geographical or popular sense, the United States that it applied to "bays" not more than six marine miles between headlands. The question was argued ably and with great learning. The tribunal appears to have been adequately informed concerning varied and significant practices affecting the status of particular bays, each according to its need. It indulged some wise observations concerning the varying bases of national interest. Nevertheless, reaching for a single formula of universal application and finding none, it came up in its award with this: "In case of bays the three marine miles are to be measured from a straight line drawn across the body of water at the place where it ceases to have the configuration and characteristics of a bay." The decision was admittedly unsatisfactory, but it was thought to be "correct in principle and the only one possible in view of the want of a sufficient basis for a more concrete answer." Fortunately the tribunal had authority to make recommendations and it opened the way to an eventual adjustment by appending some which were largely accepted. On the question actually decided, however, there was needless retreat in the presence of an assumed lacuna, no credit to judicial statecraft, and no contribution to much needed confidence in the processes of arbitration.

More of judicial statecraft is observed in the award of another arbitral tribunal made the preceding year in the Grisbadarna Case between Norway and Sweden. It was a boundary case. The boundary between the two nations had been settled to the sea but in the marginal sea was in dispute. The disputed seas were studded with isles, banks, and reefs. Among other things valuable fishing banks were at stake. An arbitral tribunal was established and it was agreed that it should "determine the boundary-line

. . . up to the limit of the territorial waters." In so determining, it was to take into account "the circumstances of fact and the principles of international law." Needless to say, the circumstances of fact were unique, there were no precedents precisely in point, and there was no single principle universally approved and clearly applicable. Had there been, there would have been no need for arbitration. Surely there must have been strong temptation to detour in the presence of assumed gaps or lacunae. But there was no detouring. Judicial responsibility had been imposed and the tribunal proceeded to discharge it, saying: "In the first place, the tribunal is of opinion that the clause in accordance with which it is to determine the boundary-line in the sea as far as the limit of the territorial waters has no other purpose than to exclude the possibility of an incomplete determination, which might give rise to a new boundary dispute in future."

The tribunal proceeded to make a complete determination after exploring analogies, excluding inapplicable rules, and ultimately formulating an applicable rule thought to be in harmony with principle and in accord with the facts. A line midway the inhabited islands was found insufficiently supported in international law of the decisive period. The rule of the *thalweg* or main channel was inapplicable. Sufficiently supported, on the other hand, was a line projected "perpendicularly to the general direction of the coast, while taking into account the necessity of indicating the boundary in a clear and unmistakable manner." Approval of this latter line gave the Grisbadarna banks to Sweden. The tribunal was satisfied that Swedes had utilized these banks earlier, more effectively and longer. Moreover, Sweden had placed beacons, measured depths and installed a light-boat. "It is a settled principle of the law of nations," said the tribunal, "that a state of things which actually exists and has existed for a long time should be changed as little as possible." The broad statement referred, of course, to the "state of things" which had actually existed with respect to the Grisbadarna. The decision was something less than epoch making, no doubt, but it settled a dispute, added useful precedent, and left a record of judicial work well done. In the progressive accumulation of such decisions the law grows, interstitially if you please, but significantly over the years.

We promised also some examples of contrasting failure and success from the field of law-making by agreement. There is time for one such contrast. To date we have had failure with respect to the width of territorial waters. The most notable recent effort was at the Conference for the Codification of International Law at The Hague in 1930. There had been extensive preparatory studies. Participating governments had been invited to state their views and had done so. Their delegates had then assembled to restate the same views and stand firm against any others. Opinion being "much divided" among proponents of a three-mile, four-mile, six-mile, or other widths, no agreement upon a single width could be reached. Is it just possible that it was a mistake to expend so much effort in search of agreement on a single width which disparate factual bases might largely fail to support? It was acknowledged at the Conference that "these differences of opinion were to a great extent the result of the varying geographical and economic conditions in different States and parts of the world." Were there perhaps other bases or techniques of reconciliation which might have enabled the Conference to fill out a gap instead of reporting a failure?

Recent experience in extending the international law of commercial air navigation would seem to suggest an affirmative answer. Few major problems could have been more difficult than this one was in the setting of the years at the end of the second World War. Those who were thinking primarily in terms of a universal code were predicting failure; but a universal code, as the International Civil Aviation Conference at Chicago was to demonstrate, was not the only way. The Conference produced a general convention containing as much as all could agree upon. That, to be sure, was not much, though permanent organization, procedure, and the standardization of technical practices were well covered. In addition to the general Convention on International Civil Aviation there were produced also an optional Transit Agreement extending "two freedoms" to scheduled air services and an optional Transport Agreement extending "five freedoms." Thus areas of present agreement were organized usefully and the way was opened for a progressive extension of such areas. The present system, consisting as it does of a general agreement, optional supplementary agreements, and a network of bilateral agreements and national laws, may appear to be more than a little complicated. Perhaps, if so, it is complicated in necessary adjustment to the complicated facts of international life. In any event, it is flexible, it works, and it encourages a useful development. Over the more troublesome gaps there are now bridges which may be widened and strengthened with the passing of time.

IV

In our survey of the international practice which is concerned chiefly with the national domain, we have been impressed among other things by the pretensions of sovereignty and the obstacles which they present to the development of order. Indeed, few features are more characteristic of the international system in all its parts. Yet how defective a system in which order must always bow out backward, so to speak, in the presence of sovereignty!

When nations lived in a state of nature there was no help for it. Nor were exaggerations wholly without virtue. Sovereignty was a sort of ideological defense against improper interference by one in the affairs of another. In proportion as its pretensions were acknowledged, it was protection for the weak against the strong. With an expanding consciousness of common interest, however, and with improvements in the organization of international coöperation, the justifying occasions have occurred less frequently. Often the old habits have persisted for no better reason than that they are old habits. Are there means of growth? Again it will be helpful to look at some illustrative decisions and also to consider at least an instance or two of progress by agreement.

In the case of the steamship "David," decided in 1933 in an arbitration between Panama and the United States, there is a striking illustration of what old habits can do to frustrate the processes of realistic judicial adjustment. There had been a collision off the coast of Panama between the Panamanian steamship "David" and the American steamship "Yorba Linda." As is not infrequently the case in such circumstances, each charged the other with fault. The Panamanian owner sued the American owner in a court of Panama, the defendant neither appearing nor responding, and recovered a judgment in the sum of approximately $27,000. The American owner thereupon libeled the "David" *in rem,* as lawyers say, in a court of the Canal Zone, and had the "David" arrested by the United States Marshal while the vessel was passing along the coast on a voyage from one port of Panama to another. Whether the arrest was made within or without the Canal Zone's three-mile limit was disputed. Even if made within, it was strongly contended, it was made while the vessel was in innocent passage, and hence not subject to arrest by United States authorities in a civil suit. The Panamanian owner put up a bond for the release of the "David" and the several suits were later compromised by an agreement whereby the American owner paid the Panamanian owner some $16,000 in settlement. In behalf of the Panamanian owner, Panama asked an indemnity of the United States, contending that the arrest of the "David" was in violation of international law and had compelled the Panamanian owner to give bond to his detriment and to agree to a settlement which he would not otherwise have accepted. There was thus presented a clear issue as to whether under international law a foreign ship may be subjected to civil arrest while in innocent passage through territorial waters.

It was decided, the Panamanian Commissioner dissenting, that the "David" was not exempt from civil arrest under the rule of innocent passage. Other and more competent bodies, public and private, had explored the same general question previously and had reached a contrary conclusion, but there was negligible precedent. As always, there was sovereignty! Sovereignty, it would seem, was capable of preventing this or any other tribunal from creating the first useful precedent. Speaking for its majority, the Commission said: "The general rule of the extension of sovereignty over the three-mile zone is clearly established. Exceptions to the completeness of this sovereignty should be supported by clear authority. There is a clear preponderance of authority to the effect that this sovereignty is qualified by what is known as the right of innocent passage, and that this qualification forbids the sovereign actually to prohibit the innocent passage of alien merchant vessels through its territorial waters. There is no clear preponderance of authority to the effect that such vessels when passing through territorial waters are exempt from civil arrest. In the absence of such authority, the Commission cannot say that a country may not, under the rules of international law, assert the right to arrest on civil process merchant ships passing through its territorial waters."

Needless to say, we are here concerned chiefly with the reasoning, and not with a particular rule. The rule announced may have been bad enough, but the reasoning was infinitely worse. Too often repeated, such reaffirmations of the ancient anarchy could frustrate all prospect of a truly progressive development through judicial decisions. Fortunately there are other decisions which present the international arbitral or judicial process in a more favorable light. We may select one which also exposes more clearly the elemental truth that in the nature of most international controversy some aspect of the sovereignty of one nation is in collision with some aspect of the sovereignty of another. Once this truth is fully appreciated, such grandiose premises as those invoked in the case of the steamship "David" become largely irrelevant, and we are ready to get on with the work of judicial accommodation.

The case of the North American Dredging Company of Texas was before the general claims tribunal set up pursuant to the Convention concluded between Mexico and the United States in 1923. The company had obtained from the Mexican Government in Mexico in 1912 a contract for the dredging of a Mexican port. An essential provision of the contract, as in all such contracts procured south of the Rio Grande, was an article stipulating that the contractor should have or claim in connection with the contract only such rights or remedies as were assured Mexicans under Mexican law in similar circumstances and that under no circumstances should there be diplomatic interposition. This was the so-called "Calvo clause" to which our neighbors south of the Rio Grande attach generally so much importance, and which we in turn have viewed with so much misgiving. In consequence of Mexico's alleged breaches of this contract, the company claimed heavy losses and damages. Apparently with little or no regard for the remedies which the Mexican law may have afforded, the company sought and obtained the interposition of the United States in its behalf. There was an article in the Convention of 1923 which provided that "no claim shall be disallowed or rejected by the Commission by the application of the general principle of international law that the legal remedies must be exhausted as a condition precedent to the validity or allowance of any claim." Notwithstanding this stipulation, Mexico moved to dismiss the case. The effect of the "Calvo clause" was thus put in issue.

In argument Mexico made much of its "sovereign right" of jurisdiction within its territory, the United States much of its "sovereign right" to protect a national abroad. The Commission was not greatly impressed with these arguments, particularly when they were pressed to extremes. It said: "The present stage of international law imposes upon every international tribunal the solemn duty of seeking for a proper and adequate balance between the sovereign right of national jurisdiction, on the one hand, and the sovereign right of national protection of citizens on the other. No international tribunal should or may evade the task of finding such limitations of both rights as will render them compatible within the general rules and principles of international law." There was observed in the "Calvo clause" an attempt to draw a reasonable and practical line between these competing rights. While conceding that the clause could not exclude the right of the United States to interpose after international law had been violated, the Commission thought that it could exclude interposition for mere breach of contract in advance of any recourse to local remedies. And it could do so notwithstanding the article in the Convention of 1923 which we have quoted. Each case involving the "Calvo clause" should be decided on its merits and not on sweeping generalizations as to sovereignty. On the case presented, the claim was dismissed.

Again, it is not a rule of decision with which we are chiefly concerned. It is an approach, a manner of reasoning, a process. There will always be those who think that a tribunal has gone too far, or that it has not gone far enough, or that it has been ill-advised. That is all in the day's work. What is important is that international tribunals accept full responsibility for judicial accommodation in every case and that they refuse to be intimidated by the pretensions of sovereignty. When they do as much, the way is assuredly open to useful development. The means of growth are at hand.

There will be situations, however, in which development of the law through decisions is much too restricted and too slow. Novel situations may get completely out of hand in the absence of something equivalent to legislation. So, dramatically enough, of the international regulation of atomic energy. Or less than novel situations may have been dallied with so long that eventually they explode in circumstances calling for a comprehensive solution. So, in comparable drama, of the international protection of minorities against extermination. Or, without drama, a matter of common interest to a considerable number of nations may simply have become ripe for common regulation. As we have noted hitherto, the recourse in such situations is to law-making by agreement. It will come as no surprise that agreement, like decision, may be and frequently is obstructed by the pretensions of sovereignty. This is not to suggest that every proposed agreement should override the pretensions. Not infrequently there may be proposals which would undertake too much. It is to suggest that the arguments concerning agreement, like those concerning decision, should be premised upon the realities of national interest or necessity and not upon a concept. Unless they are so premised, there is poor prospect that bases of reconciliation will be found.

In the matter of atomic energy, the nations are struggling at this moment with something that is at once unprecedented and extremely urgent. Unless agreements can be made and implemented, the situation may get dangerously out of hand. The official proposals of the Western powers have been in effect proposals for a kind of world government in a dangerous area. It is urged that nothing less will succeed. As must have been anticipated, reactions have been varied and violent. As must have been anticipated, also, we have heard a good deal about sovereignty. Some have talked of surrendering it for general security. Others will have no part in such surrender. The clash is unfortunately part of a larger crisis which must be resolved before much progress can be made. Of this only we may be sure. The conditions of reconciliation which may ultimately be exploited successfully will be conditions of substance and not mere exaggerations of an idea.

As regards the international protection of minorities against extermination, the procedures of agreement are farther along and the prospects of an early success are more favorable. Before the nations for ratification at the present time, after unanimous approval by the General Assembly of the United Nations, is the Convention on the Prevention and Punishment of the Crime of Genocide. There will be critics of this instrument of agreement, no doubt, but surely there will be none to take credit for the centuries of dallying when brutalities were defended in terms of sovereign irresponsibility and only the grossest excesses provoked protests on grounds of humanity. Hitler's extermination camps brought an awakening. The Charter of the International Military Tribunal denounced crimes against humanity. The General Assembly declared genocide a crime under international law. And now the Convention, after patient and prolonged effort, has spelled out the offense and made a cautious beginning with procedures.

These two instances of progress by agreement, the one still in hope and the other perhaps nearing realization, have been highly dramatic. There has also been a good deal of such progress in less exciting areas and without drama, notably in the course of the last generation. Judge Hudson's *International Legislation* is a repository of examples. Often the pretensions of sovereignty have delayed, compelled detours, or blocked the way to mutual advantage. Much real progress has been made, nevertheless, and it is clear that the procedures and techniques developed in this experience have become important means of growth within the patterns of an existing order.

V

Important gaps, or lacunae, and exaggerations of sovereignty appear also in the law and practice of jurisdiction —the fourth grand aspect of the subject to be reconnoitered—though in some respects they are less characteristic here than elsewhere. In any case, in reconnoitering jurisdiction we have been more impressed by conflicts among the national systems, by the frequent exaggerations of what appear to be essentially superficial differences, and by a significant progress in accommodation and the development of techniques of reconciliation. At the national level, legislatures have implemented from time to time in an accepted pattern and where the need was obvious have even aimed at uniformity. At the international level there have been some significant achievements in law-making by agreement. National courts have developed significant reconciliation techniques, notably in matters of maritime and private international law. Where international tribunals have been created and used, it has become increasingly evident that there are comparably serviceable techniques which may be cultivated to advantage. As much may be illustrated by reference to a conflict of penal jurisdictions which once provoked a famous incident and which has been argued more recently in a famous case. Contrasting incident and decision, we may observe both the anarchy of undisciplined conflict and the growth of legal order.

In 1886, a national of the United States, one Cutting, was engaged in editing a newspaper in Paso del Norte, Mexico. Having attacked in print the character and good faith of one Medina, a Mexican, who had proposed to start a rival newspaper in the same town, Cutting was arrested to stand trial on Medina's complaint for an offense in the nature of criminal libel. The parties were brought into court, something called a "reconciliation" in Mexican practice was accepted and signed before the local judge, and the "reconciliation" was published in Cutting's newspaper. Medina thereupon withdrew his complaint and the case was dismissed. Cutting then crossed the international boundary to El Paso, Texas, took space in an El Paso newspaper, and reiterated with some embellishments his former charges against Medina. Upon his return to Paso del Norte, Cutting was again arrested and was committed to stand trial, as the Mexican law permitted, for an offense against a Mexican in a foreign country. The United States took the matter up highly, demanding the "instant release" of Cutting and repeal of the Mexican law under which he had been held to stand trial.

It was not questioned that Cutting might have been tried in Mexico for circulating the libel in Mexico. Indeed, there was abundant precedent in the United States in support of such a conclusion. Presumably he could have been tried also for breach of the "reconciliation" on reasoning supported by our own notions concerning contempt of court. But the Secretary of State of the United States contended vigorously, if not violently, that the courts of Mexico were completely incapable under international law of trying a United States national for an offense committed in the United States merely because the object of the offense happened to be a Mexican. Strong language was used and there was a prolonged period of tension. Mexico stood its ground, relying upon a principle rarely invoked but supported by provisions in a number of national penal codes. After Mexican contentions had been reaffirmed in decisions of the Mexican courts, the complaint was withdrawn and Cutting was released, apparently to relieve the tension. Nothing was settled. It is generally assumed that the contentions thus advanced are still the contentions of Mexico and the United States respectively.

Forty years later, in 1926, there was a collision on the high seas between a French steamer, the "Lotus," and a Turkish collier, the "Boz-Kourt," in which the Turkish collier was sunk and eight Turkish sailors or passengers on the unfortunate vessel were drowned. When the French steamer arrived at Constantinople with the survivors, Lieutenant Demons, the French officer of the watch on the "Lotus" at the time of the collision, was arrested, tried, and convicted on a charge of involuntary manslaughter. France denounced these proceedings as in conflict with principles of international law and demanded Lieutenant Demons' release. By special agreement between France and Turkey, the question of jurisdiction thus raised was submitted to the Permanent Court of International Justice. The agreement did not indicate specific Turkish legislation upon which the prosecution had been based, but much was made in argument of Article 6 of the Turkish Penal Code, similar to the Mexican law upon which Cutting's prosecution had been based forty years before, and providing with important limitations for the prosecution of a foreigner for an offense committed abroad to the prejudice of a Turkish subject.

The Court concluded that conformity of Article 6 with principles of international law was not at issue. The question was a more general one, viz., whether there were any rules of international law which had been violated by the Turkish proceedings. Even if Article 6 were considered not in conformity, there were other provisions invulnerable to criticism. Assimilating the Turkish ship to Turkish territory, it was observed that the offense had been consummated within Turkish territorial authority. Limitations upon such authority were not to be presumed. They had not been proved and certainly there were no restrictive rules peculiar to collision cases. "Once it is admitted," said the prevailing opinion, "that the effects of the offense were produced on the Turkish vessel, it becomes impossible to hold that there is a rule of international law which prohibits Turkey from prosecuting Lieutenant Demons because of the fact that the author of the offense was on board the French ship." The Court being equally divided in opinion, it was decided by the President's casting vote that Turkey had not acted in violation of international law.

Thus we are assured, in so far as assurance can come from an evenly divided court, that international law does not prohibit the localization of involuntary manslaughter where the mortal effect is produced. We are further assured that such localization may be made on a ship in case of collision on the high seas between ships sailing under different flags. We still do not know what an international court may conclude when an issue is presented as to penal jurisdiction based exclusively upon the nationality of the aggrieved person. Though certain of the Court's premises are vulnerable to professional criticism and some of its conclusions will continue to be debated, particularly among shipowners and their attorneys, the significant thing is that the matter was resolved under law. The period of tension was short. The adjustment was orderly. Old precedents and reasonings were reëxamined and the ways to progress through judicial decision were freshly illumined. Better a multiplicity of juridical doubts stemming from such an adjustment than a single Cutting crisis. If like processes may be perfected and more widely used, it need be no daydream to envisage the jurisdiction of nations as system and order where the disorders of exaggerated conflict have hitherto prevailed.

While the growth that endures will probably be fostered largely in comparable judicial experience, at both the national and the international level, there will also be areas of jurisdictional conflict which may be harmonized by the more embracing processes of made law. Accord by agreement has its role. There has accumulated an experience which, though halting and meager, is enough to point the way. As hitherto suggested, a little has been accomplished among groups of nations within the larger community in matters maritime, in private international law and elsewhere. Techniques similarly developed in harmonizing important substantive practices are applicable to jurisdictional problems. Perhaps no cleavage is sharper or more fundamental today than that observed between Communist countries and the Western Democracies with respect to the function of a court. Yet it was possible, in framing the Charter of the International Military Tribunal which sat at Nuremberg, to compromise even this cleavage. If great nations may become as concerned to build for an enduring peace through law as they were to punish war criminals after the last great war, it would appear that bases of legal order may be found. The means of growth are at hand. It is only the firm purpose that is frustrated for a time in the babel of frightened and discordant voices.

VI

Vital relationships left largely to an unregulated political adjustment, gaps persisting where accepted principles are needed, sovereignty magnified to frustrate an essential coöperation, and conflicts stressed where reconciliation is attainable—these are among the shortcomings which a reinvigorated jurisprudence should be able to outgrow. When we come to the international law of agreements, we are impressed with none of these defects so much as with the subject's apparent paradoxes: procedural maturity and timidities of use, reliable methods of interpretation and persisting controversies about meaning, *pacta sunt servanda* and agreements made under duress. Perhaps the apparent paradoxes are no more than further aspects of the same basic phenomenon: a world groping reluctantly in uncertainty and fear to escape the consequences of its anarchy through improvement of its organization. In any case, as we have noted elsewhere, there are opportunities for growth which the nations have hardly begun to exploit.

Thus practice has long since made available a wide variety of methods and forms of agreement adapted to expeditious use with respect to any and every matter of international concern. That is almost as far as any system of law can go. Except as it may restrict and regulate the alternatives to agreement—of which more will be said presently—law can ordinarily do little more than provide the means and facilitate the processes. Here international law has not done badly. The will to agree is obviously another matter.

Thus, also, the practice in modern times has developed liberal and enlightened principles to govern the interpretation of agreements. Between the two great wars, contributions of the Permanent Court of International Justice were notable. The so-called optional clause in the Statute of that Court and in the Statute of the present International Court of Justice has placed first among the legal disputes appropriate for a compulsory jurisdiction without special agreement such controversies as concern "the interpretation of a treaty." More than half the nations which are parties to the Statute have now accepted the obligations of the optional clause by declarations in varying terms. The way is open, it would appear, for a relatively mature legal development so far as the making and the interpreting of international agreements may be concerned. This is not to say that there is law enough or that the law we have is good enough. It is to say that there are resources of growth which may be cultivated much more boldly. Obviously the law of agreements is of fundamental importance in the struggle for order.

May not the same resources of growth encompass the more difficult problems of termination for breach or termination in consequence of changed conditions? The Statute of the International Court of Justice places second among legal disputes suitable for compulsory adjudication, after disputes concerning "the interpretation of a treaty," disputes concerning "any question of international law." Surely these problems, whatever the political setting, are preëminently problems of treaty interpretation and international law. Imperfect though they may be, we have institutions and procedures and we have a substantial commitment to their use. It would appear that the traditional anarchy and violence in these matters have no excuse except as excuse may be sought deliberately outside the law.

Our country's first formal international agreements were incorporated in treaties with France in 1778. The subsequent history of these treaties is a narrative which illustrates the traditional anarchy. It was contended that our Jay Treaty of 1794 with Britain was in conflict with our earlier obligations to France. There were charges and countercharges, and in the period of revolution and war which was soon sweeping over Europe the shipping and trade of the young republic of the Western Hemisphere were roughly and contemptuously handled. In 1798, reciting that the French treaties had been repeatedly violated, that just claims for reparation had been refused, and that attempts to negotiate an amicable settlement had been repelled with indignity, the Congress of the United States formally abrogated the earlier agreements. There followed an undeclared war with France from which the United States eventually emerged without major disaster largely because of the preoccupation of the great powers with the contest in Europe. In the aftermath of adjustment and domestic settlement of claims alleged to have been assumed by the United States, the termination of agreements for breach and in consequence of changed conditions were debated inconclusively for nearly one hundred years.

Today, with France and the United States parties to the optional clause of the Statute of the International Court of Justice, such a controversy should be on its way to definitive adjustment under law within one hundred days. The Permanent Court of International Justice, in opinions which will undoubtedly guide the present International Court, has indicated clearly and correctly that such matters are appropriate for adjudication according to law. The procedures and the techniques are at hand.

Most disturbing of the paradoxes observed in this division of our subject, no doubt, is the one stressed in placing side by side the propositions that agreements are binding and that agreements made under duress are as good as any other. Actually agreements made under duress are no better and are not likely to be more enduring than the force which compels acquiescence. Basically, it would seem, this is not a problem of the law of agreements. Rather it is a problem of the law of adjustment. Its solutions are to be found in provisions for decent and orderly alternatives where agreements cannot be made freely and in the substitution of organized force for individual coercion where coercion becomes ultimately necessary. So we pass on to see what there is of viability and vigor in contemporary practice with respect to the adjustment of international disputes.

VII

It is in the law and practice of adjustment and its orderly alternatives to violence that the prospects for a healthy development within the patterns of the existing international system are least encouraging. Concede that a traditional theory of war as regulated trial of right has passed into limbo, that war as an instrument of national policy has been renounced, and that wars of aggression have become international crimes. While some may doubt, there is much to support these concessions. Recall that sixty nations are now pledged in the first article of the United Nations Charter "to maintain international peace and security, and to that end: to take effective collective measures for the prevention and removal of threats to the peace, and for the suppression of acts of aggression or other breaches of the peace, and to bring about by peaceful means, and in conformity with the principles of justice and international law, adjustment or settlement of international disputes or situations which might lead to a breach of the peace." There persists the dichotomy of adjustment by recourse to so-called "amicable modes" and to "non-amicable modes short of war." If some of the traditional "non-amicable modes" have been renounced, to the extent at least that good resolutions can make renunciation effective, it would appear realistically that we must now add to the grim category of non-amicable methods the modern techniques of hostile propaganda, infiltration, and subversion. So long as any substantial measure of self-help is permitted to persist, whether in its crasser or its subtler forms, there is chronic danger of the condition of war. International war in our time may have become a kind of civil war, a revolt against organized international order, but its devastations are no less real. No doubt there are gains in theory which have a long-term significance; but such gains, when self-help is permitted to degenerate into armed conflict, will neither restore the desolating waste nor return the dead. One is tempted to say, in familiar phrase, that it is a condition and not a theory which confronts us.

It may be observed that there are prospects of further growth in the means and methods of negotiation, notwithstanding their tested maturity. The procedures and the techniques of conciliation, arbitration, and adjudication are rudimentary but healthy. Who shall doubt that a sturdier and vastly more useful development might be achieved if there were less of timidity, more of consciously creative effort and a bold extension of such methods of adjustment through fructifying use. It is in bold and constant use that virtues are discovered, defects revealed, and ways opened for serviceable extension of the legal order. Something of all this is illustrated, with indication of some important unfinished business, in a case recently before the International Court of Justice.

The Corfu Channel off the Albanian coast constitutes a part of the frontier between Albania and Greece and also serves as an important coastwise waterway between the Ionian and the Adriatic seas. Much of the waterway is wholly within the territorial waters of Albania or Greece. Late in the recent war, in October-November 1944, the Channel was swept clear of mines by the British Navy and the existence of a safe route was announced. In January-February 1945 it was check-swept with like results. In May 1946 British warships passed safely through without special precautions. On October 22, 1946, while a squadron of British warships was proceeding through the Channel, two destroyers struck contact mines in Albanian territorial waters. There were explosions which caused damage to the destroyers and heavy loss of life. On November 12-13, 1946, notwithstanding Albanian protest, the British Navy swept the Channel again and discovered a newly laid field of anchored mines at the place where the explosions of October 22 had occurred.

The United Kingdom charged Albania with responsibility. The case came before the International Court of Justice under a special agreement of March 25, 1948, submitting for decision questions as to whether Albania was responsible under international law and obligated to pay compensation and whether the United Kingdom had violated Albanian sovereignty in its use of the Channel and in its mine-sweeping operations in Albanian territorial waters without Albanian consent. A majority of the Court were of opinion that warships were entitled to an innocent passage through the Channel and that Albania was responsible for the explosions and resulting damage and loss of life. The Court was unanimously of opinion that the mine-sweeping operations of November 12-13, 1946, without Albania's consent, were a violation of sovereignty. The Court's declaration on this latter point was considered in itself an appropriate satisfaction.

Thus a major controversy between a great nation and a small one was judicially adjusted. In the adjustment there was useful illumination of the principles governing innocent passage through such a waterway. There were contributions to methods of proof, inferences from evidence and the broader principles of national responsibility. One need not be highly proficient in the techniques of law to detect also in the result an intriguing paradox which points up some unfinished business in the continuing task of building legal order. In its mine-sweeping in territorial waters over Albania's protest, the United Kingdom had violated sovereignty. On this there was no dissent. Yet, by eleven votes to five, the same Court found Albania responsible for the explosions and for the resulting damage and loss of life on evidence obtained by the mine-sweeping. Self-help was condemned, but the fruits thereof were rewarded. This is not to suggest that justice could have been better administered under existing circumstances. It is to suggest that international organization clearly requires a more effective implementing and a further development to the end that facts may be known and justice administered without hazardous resort to self-help to confirm a well-founded suspicion.

We shall not go over again the deficiencies of the exist ing institutions of international adjustment as reviewed in a preceding essay. It is plain that they are inadequate. Until every international dispute may be disposed of readily, in orderly recourse to institutions organized and available and by processes in which there is a widespread confidence, it is clear that self-help with all its attendant perils must continue to bedevil the good neighborhood of peoples.

VIII

In summary, the prospect for a useful growth of international law is observed in lights and shadows. We have emphasized the lights a little because, in times of tension, there is a tendency to see only the frustrating shades. In matters reserved traditionally for political accommodation, such as the birth, recognition, life, and death of a nation, there are germinal practices in the existing system which have potentialities as yet but slightly cultivated. Nor are the familiar gaps or lacunae of international law irremediable, even with the restricted resources of the contemporary community, as we have endeavored to demonstrate. A constructive view of the function of decision under law may accomplish much; and a fresh approach to codification and the progressive development of the law, with careful attention to the disparate factual bases of national interest, may achieve more. Sovereignty in its manifold extravagances is an understandable consequence of the insecurity of national life in a community so imperfectly integrated. It is also a shibboleth. There is ample opportunity, as has been illustrated, for a progressive mitigation of its excesses. Ultimately its subordination to the general welfare will be in proportion to the increase of security through improvements in organization. The conflicts which are characteristic in matters of jurisdiction stem more often than otherwise from national differences which are superficial, or which may be narrowly defined, and their reconciliation awaits only a more insistent recourse to proven techniques. Even the conflicts which are fundamental may be reconciled if available techniques are exploited boldly. The law of agreements presents a rich experience awaiting bolder cultivation. It also presents problems whose solution will require a firmer organization of the legal order. The institutions which provide alternatives to agreement, in lieu of self-help, are patently inadequate. While growth could be greatly stimulated by a more courageous recourse to what we have, it is here conspicuously that better organization must correct the more dangerous deficiencies. The needed improvements in organization which are here so obvious will do more than fortify and perfect the law of adjustment. They will greatly vitalize the resources of growth which have been observed elsewhere in an expanding system.

The Law and Peace

I

FOR OUR concluding essay, we return to the title which has been given the series. As indicated in the Foreword, this title has been deliberately chosen. "Peace under Law" as a title invites daydreaming. "Law under Peace" is surrender. "Law and Peace" should suggest the union in constructive enterprise of a condition desired and the social institution which may assure its permanence, each fortifying the other.

Law in the more embracing sense as a social institution is justified in proportion as it assures order. It is law in this sense and among members of the world society with which we are ultimately concerned. There is a world community. There is a world law. World law has yet to assure the order and decency which exclude violence and supplant anarchy. Yet of it there is a vast body that is useful, indeed indispensable, and contained in its practices and principles are great potentialities of growth. How may these potentialities be best exploited? Will it be possible to exploit them rapidly enough? Are we in race with catastrophe?

Before proceeding further, it will perhaps not come amiss to say a word about climbing haystacks. There have always been among us those who become overwrought in contemplation of the sinfulness of man, have morbid visions of terrestrial disintegration and climb on haystacks, figuratively or literally, to await the end of the world. Until now these self-appointed prophets have always been mistaken and correspondingly humiliated. Nor has their contribution to the suppression of sin ever been a useful one. It is suggested that comparable disappointments probably await those other forecasters of disaster who are currently offering us an immediate and inescapable choice between panaceas for global salvation and the disintegration of all civilization. However we may choose to regard the contemporary crisis—whether as continuation of the ageless struggle of humanity against unreason or as test without precedent of humanity's capacity to survive—some things are clear. No good can come of hysteria. There is neither comfort nor security on haystacks. The alternatives are not simple and obvious. The battle is joined everywhere on a front of extraordinary complications, no sector of which may be safely neglected. Well-advised, we shall keep and reinvigorate what we have of order, plan and project more, and always in firm determination "to establish conditions under which justice and respect for the obligations arising from treaties and other sources of international law can be maintained." Every day of peace is a time for the extension of law. Every extension of law should strengthen the condition of peace.

II

In holding on to the good in what we have and pressing forward with its reinvigoration and extension, it is suggested that we may profitably begin by reëxamining the institutions and processes of administration, particularly judicial administration. Needless to say, law is not likely to be much better than its administration. A combination of bad law and bad administration is the nadir of juristic achievement. Good law and bad administration are but little better. Bad law and good administration may accomplish more, though rarely enough. The objective, of course, is always good law and the wise and understanding judge. It is not often that such formulae are quite descriptive of the whole and certainly no one of them can be applied comprehensively to the jurisprudence of nations. Of international law, one may say perhaps that considering the circumstances of its development it is surprising that so much is good. Of its institutions of administration, it must be said that they remain primitive and incomplete.

Reëxamination will suggest accordingly, among other things, an urgent need for the extension and improvement of what may be called the international judicial system. We have now in the International Court of Justice, successor to the Permanent Court of International Justice, a high court of international law whose jurisdiction has been progressively extended in a multiplicity of treaty provisions and whose work has progressively gained confidence in the generation of its service. The necessary structure of specialized, intermediate, or trial tribunals remains characteristically *ad hoc* and impermanent. Thus the International Court sits precariously at the peak of a pyramid which has no enduring base. To say that the institutions of which the pyramid consists are primitive and incomplete is to speak mildly. In consequence the law's administration falters. Its growth through administration is retarded. As stressed hitherto, whenever agreement fails there must be an orderly alternative to self-help under law administered or made. Even small disputes permitted to accumulate may become as dangerous as large disputes. The habits of adjustment under law must be sedulously cultivated. To these ends the institutions of adjustment under law should be always available, seasoned in experience, and trusted by those who resort to them.

There is clear need, therefore, for further creative effort extending the organization of international justice. Already there are areas in which the need for tribunals of a specialized competence has been indicated. There should also be tribunals of broader competence and intermediate position capable of sitting on circuit, so to speak, in continental or other natural areas of the world's unrest. A good deal of the world's legal business could be settled well enough at this level while the more novel or critical problems were carried on for consideration by the highest judicial authority. And patently there should be extended over the earth the international equivalent of national trial tribunals, permanent and always at hand, to dispose speedily of the bulk of the adjustment business as disputes arise. Until we have as much, it is difficult to see how the accumulation of lesser disputes can be prevented, the greater disputes sifted for higher consideration, or essential habits of adjustment under law firmly established. There are no insurmountable obstacles to such an extension of judicial organization. Our long experience with *ad hoc* bodies has much to contribute. The cost would be considerable, no doubt, perhaps as much initially as a few large bombers per annum.

If there is timidity of statesmanship in the presence of such an undertaking, there is an easier course which, though admittedly less satisfactory, may at least afford a valuable transitional experience. It will be recalled that the so-called Permanent Court of Arbitration, established in its present form at the Second Hague Peace Conference in 1907, provides a small administrative office, a panel of available arbitrators and an agreed procedure, and that the institution had a modest utility before the first World War. For nations which have had or are at all likely to have differences requiring adjustment, particularly the run-of-the-mine differences which are so largely suitable for adjustment according to law, it should be practicable to make similar institutions readily available through a regime of bilateral treaties patterned after the convention establishing the Court of Arbitration. If such bilateral conventions were coupled with firm and reasonably comprehensive commitments as to jurisdiction, the prospects of prompt and continuing judicial settlement of a very large part of the lesser controversies which now irritate the relations of nations would be greatly improved. Claims in behalf of nationals, for example, might be more consistently adjusted while the claimants are still alive. There might even develop such habits of adjustment as would contribute much to dispel irresolution with respect to a more effective and enduring judicial structure.

Firm and reasonably comprehensive commitments as to jurisdiction would be indispensable, needless to say, if justice under law were to be extended as the need required.

At the same time, there should also be a bold extension of national commitments as regards the jurisdiction of the International Court of Justice. Do we really want justice under law in so-called "legal disputes"? Do we really believe in the resolutions of the United Nations Charter? At the present time somewhat more than half the nations parties to the Court's Statute have accepted compulsory jurisdiction under the optional clause by declarations in varying terms and with varying reservations. Here is a "gap" which has been deliberately created and which should be promptly and effectively closed. Here is a way which should be cleared to that "juster justice and more lawful law" which most of mankind so earnestly desires.

Finally, of all tribunals participating in judicial administration, whether *ad hoc* or permanent, there should be demanded in no uncertain terms an administration "in conformity with the principles of justice and international law." This means that traditional lacunae must be spanned as necessary and that at least the more extravagant pretensions of sovereignty must be rejected. It means that techniques of reconciliation must be resolutely extended and the traditional paradoxes resolved. There should be an end of weasel-worded escapes from responsibility and of surrender to the premises of traditional disorder. Where new precedents need to be created, as the result may require, let them be created in conformity with principle and with candor and courage.

III

As we hold fast to the good while pressing on with reinvigoration and extension, it is clear that we shall need also to wage peace increasingly through made law on a more comprehensive scale. The law in custom is tough law, a firm core for the more embracing system, but it grows glacially. Even as supplemented by treaties in the nineteenth century, it became insufficient for a dynamic and changing world. Without the destruction of two world wars, the need must have become increasingly apparent. With such destruction, it has become world-wide and demanding. In building peace, therefore, there is required a vast deal of conscious law-making. This is to say that a revitalized community of nations must exploit progressively and to the full its equivalents of national law-making processes.

Realism in appraisal of the community of nations, such as was attempted in the first of these essays, does not encourage an institutional perfectionism. It is unlikely that we shall have soon a global parliament, representative of all peoples, taking firm decisions by the simple device of majority vote and thus making laws to become immediately effective. Indeed, there are many of the nations in the larger community which do not themselves have such parliaments at the present time, notably where there are written constitutions imposing limitations or requiring that important laws pass subject to referendum. Short of the world state and its parliament, where shall we turn? What are the equivalents? Useful equivalents are at hand, it is confidently suggested, in the procedures and techniques of the modern conference and notably in the conference as it has been developed in contemporary international organization. There is so much drama in the so-called "veto" and in the resulting frustrations of a single agency that we are likely, for the moment at least, to miss the import and the potentialities of a more embracing institution.

The international conference, in truth, has had a notable development as an institution for the extension of law. It has had its frustrations, as we have illustrated, but it has had also its successes. There have been times when its effectiveness compared favorably with that of many a national law-making body. Where such conferences were improvised at irregular intervals in the nineteenth century, the mechanisms of permanence and continuity have now been created with corresponding increase in utility. Where earlier conferences were insufficiently prepared, the devices of preparation have been greatly strengthened. The importance of thorough and imaginative preparation, with respect to which we have learned so much from experience, can hardly be overestimated. It was in the development of conference organization and preparation that the League of Nations made some of its most valuable contributions.

There has been also a corresponding improvement in conference procedures. The earlier institution was likely to be a gathering of diplomats, much concerned with formalities, and uncompromisingly committed to the requirement of unanimity. Characteristically governments were invited to formulate their views in advance of meeting and delegations came more concerned to defend these views to the last ounce of oratory than to find useful bases of reconciliation. Experience has taught that a thorough exploration of the problem in all its aspects is better preparation than an antecedent crystallizing of national policies, that much more effective use can be made of experts, and that in quest of a useful political adjustment there is not much progress to be achieved through eloquence in the attack or the defense. Committees and sub-committees have come to be used more effectively. Majority decisions have been greatly extended. The practice of abstention, where a delegation cannot presently support but does not wish to frustrate, has been found helpful. In short, it has been demonstrated that the international conference can be made both a continuing and a consciously responsible body in this vital area of international endeavor.

Finally, it has been discovered that there are other forms of useful conference action where it is not possible to obtain immediate and general agreement on a draft convention or treaty to be submitted to governments for ratification. There are circumstances in which a report, a resolution, a renunciation, or a declaration may be used to advantage. Soundly conceived and well timed, such forms of action may have enduring significance. War criminals were convicted and hanged at the end of the late war in considerable reliance upon an evolution of legal thought largely evidenced in such pronouncements. Who shall say that the Universal Declaration of Human Rights approved by the General Assembly of the United Nations in December of 1948 is mere phrase-making because it attempts no more than the formulation of "a common standard of achievement"? That would be myopia indeed. Increasingly we learn that there are many ways of getting on with the building of a better order. None should be neglected.

The better order called peace will be built of law in all its ramifications. In pressing on with improvement of the law's administration and with a more forthright extension of its rule, we cannot wait for an international constitutional convention. There may come a time for such an assembling, but meanwhile we must use and develop the institutions at hand to better advantage. The institutions available will not work miracles, but they are capable nevertheless of strengthening peace in an infinity of ways.

You are thinking, perhaps, of the terrifying possibilities of atomic warfare and of the frustration of current attempts to forestall it. Must we not attempt more? Until this dread force is regulated, what good in all the rest? If such is the direction of your thought, it may be worth your while to reflect further upon two important questions. First: would solution for this new and compelling problem be measurably easier in a parliament of man? Who can know? Second: may not the increments of confidence which it is within our capacity to win everywhere, on a vast and complicated front, contribute as much in the end as the grand strategy of frontal attack? Who can be sure? It is just possible that we are in danger of oversimplifying the solution of a major problem while neglecting the multiplicity of ways in which its perils may be reduced and insulated.

IV

While exploiting the multiplicity of ways, it seems apparent that the cause of peace in this troubled century may be advanced as well by a reëxamination of objectives. Old objectives may be retained consciously or unconsciously. If taken for granted too long, they may become an invisible autocracy. Outmoded but still potent, they may retard or frustrate. There are some evidences of this, it is suggested, in the relationships served by international law. Without attempting anything so ambitious as an overall survey, we shall comment upon three traditional assumptions, still potent, which appear to have been considerably eroded in recent experience and to be ripe for a substantial reconsideration.

The first is an assumption, more often implicit than expressed, that to build peace we must begin by preventing war and that to prevent war we must concentrate upon the organizing of prohibitions and alternatives at the highest level. There has been something of this, implicit if not expressed, in much of the modern effort to outlaw war. It has been a motivating factor in the failures and successes of some of our "peace" conferences. Perhaps the most striking of the successes with respect to which it shares a well-earned credit has been the creation of a high court at the top of a nonexistent pyramid of institutions for judicial accommodation.

The vice in this assumption is that it proliferates partial effort where whole effort is imperative. Thus it has encouraged recourse to fiat or resolution where firm institutions and their tested processes are required. It has raised hopes soon to be frustrated for want of a more enduring base. It has given us a great tribunal which is less than capable of realizing the potentialities of its greatness largely because of the insecure foundations upon which its enterprise must rest. This does not mean that accommodation at the highest level should be neglected. On the contrary, there should be more of it. It does mean that building peace requires effort from top to bottom. Reflecting upon some aspects of the task, one is tempted to say from bottom to top. Clearly the overall objective must be something better coördinated and more nearly complete. Work on the foundations may be more arduous and less dramatic, but ultimately such work must be done and done well if confidence is to be cultivated and the good order extended.

The second is an assumption, retarding significantly the extension of useful law among nations, that acceptable rules or principles must operate upon like subjects and situations the same everywhere. Implicitly or expressly, it aims at uniformity and universality. The objectives become one for all and all for one. There is a core of solid truth in these ideas but it is not the whole truth, as experience should have reminded. Actually, on this complicated earth, there can never be an adequate and comprehensive system of laws which have the same impact upon all nations and peoples at all times. So it has happened that in conscious or unconscious quest of uniformity of rule we have been constrained frequently to rest with a modicum of general principle which is widely accepted while leaving even more important relationships to the conflict of diverging national ideas or doctrines. So it has happened that nations, particularly the more powerful nations, have striven to enforce upon others the principles of conduct which have seemed good to them. Much of all this has been vain. Most of it has been unnecessary. Uniformity is not the one and only goal. It is suggested that its more uncompromising assumptions are ripe for reëxamination and that such reëxamination may well point the way to a more feasible and useful extension of the legal order.

Reconsideration will begin, needless to say, with acknowledgment of the disparities of national interest which derive from real disparities of condition or circumstance. We have discussed in an earlier essay the factual bases of national interest and behavior and it will be enough here to refer to the earlier discussion. Where dissimilarities are basic or essential, it can serve no useful purpose to ignore them or to seek to deny them. There will be times when even the neatest of juridical postulates must fail to impose a uniform rule upon variations of geography, resource, population, or culture. At such times it need not be a matter of formulating one rule for all or in the alternative of abandoning the area to conflict. Rather it should become a matter of developing the techniques of reconciliation on a more comprehensive and serviceable scale. There need be no doubt that this can be done, once the task is understood and its importance appreciated.

Revision of objectives and corresponding shift of emphasis from uniformity to reconciliation, as we have learned in private international law and elsewhere, should enable us to occupy the more important lacunae and bridge the more difficult gaps. Within limitations, the effort may be advanced through constructive administration. More broadly, it will have recourse to equivalents of legislation. From it all may come ultimately more of unification than we are able to anticipate at the moment. Let us have uniformity by all means where it is well-founded and attainable. Elsewhere unification and reconciliation should go forward together, each complementing the other, remembering always that the irreducible minima of uniformity are a uniform tolerance of essential diversities and a uniform acceptance of the principles and practices of reconciliation.

The third assumption here selected for comment has

been expressed generally in the traditional formula, worn threadbare in repetition, that only nations are subjects of international law and that individual human beings are mere objects. Whatever validity the formula may have had in past times, when international relations were for the most part just such relations as the adjective "international" describes, there can be little doubt that it has lost much of its significance under modern conditions. Nor is it to be doubted that reëxamination has contributed to practical action. Some of the most influential of modern jurists have sensed a change and have attacked the old idea vigorously. The Charter begins: "We, the Peoples of the United Nations." Throughout the Charter there is an unprecedented concern for fundamental human rights and the individual's well-being. The Universal Declaration of Human Rights is in the same trend, as is the pending Genocide Convention. All this and more, yet there remains much to be cleared away or reoriented before the individual human being may be assured his rightful place and protection under a world-wide law. Perhaps, in the present state of thought and action, it is as much the persisting influence of an outmoded objective as the objective itself which requires reconsideration. An expanded concern for the individual and its effective implementing should greatly improve the old ways while opening new approaches to a better order. Certainly the time for uncritical repetition is long past. The need for constructive thought and action is apparent.

These are no more than illustrations of the invisible autocracy of objectives which have not been subjected to continuing study in the light of such conditions as are current or may be safely forecasted. The first has been elusively implicit and an influence contributing to much unbalanced effort. The second retains much virtue but requires re-study and re-formulation. As regards the third, reëxamination is currently in progress and we are able to observe a little of what this can accomplish. The illustrations are perhaps enough to point up a proposition. The proposition is that peace may be won by means of objectives as well as by action. Without sound objectives, much action may be misdirected. This we can ill-afford. In military metaphor, both the tactics and the grand strategy must be well conceived.

V

Improvements in judicial administration of the law, a progressive extension of the law into new areas, and continuing re-study of the law's objectives—these and related enterprises have centered for us in the critical post-war years in the United Nations. It could hardly be otherwise. Such enterprises are necessarily aspects of the progress of organized international coöperation. The United Nations is the principal instrument of such progress in our time. For the time, at least, there are no real alternatives. It will be well, therefore, to assess some of the accomplishments of the United Nations in these matters and to appraise the trends of a continuing effort.

As regards an improved organization of judicial administration, it must be said at the outset that the Charter of the United Nations is good as far as it goes but that it does not go far enough. The Permanent Court of International Justice has been continued as the International Court of Justice and made "the principal judicial organ of the United Nations." All members of the United Nations become *ipso facto* parties to the Statute of the Court and non-members may become parties. There are no provisions, however, for judicial organs of lesser or limited competence. While there are reiterated suggestions of recourse to other tribunals, the other tribunals remain such as the parties may improvise by means of general or special agreements. In other words, we are left to improvisation as hitherto and to all the uncertainties, delays, and confusions which must be implicit in such an arrangement.

As regards the obligation to resort to judicial adjustment and the authority of tribunals, there is a corresponding incompleteness. There are general commitments to adjust or settle international disputes by "peaceful means" and "in conformity with the principles of justice and international law." Arbitration and judicial settlement are conspicuous among the methods commended to members. Even as regards disputes important enough to warrant recourse to the International Court of Justice, however, the compulsory jurisdiction continues to be optional and thus far has been haltingly and only partially accepted. The highest court has done well with the little it has, but it is inconceivable that it could ever dispose of more than a small fraction of the matters which should be resolved by courts under law. Comparable commitments as to the lesser and more numerous disputes are conspicuously lacking. The exclusion of matters "essentially within the domestic jurisdiction" has been given a fresh and in some respects an enlarged emphasis. Justice under law is the ideal but, except for a little ground gained in behalf of the highest court, international judicial authority continues to rest largely upon such undertakings as may be improvised when decision becomes sufficiently urgent.

There is dim prospect that we shall soon obtain through such makeshifts of tribunals and jurisdiction the bridging of the gaps, the reconciliation of conflicts, and the mitigations of sovereignty which are so essential to an orderly judicial progress. There are no compelling reasons why a more coherent and effective structure of more assuring competence should not be established through the United Nations. Indeed, the truly remarkable accomplishments of the United Nations and its related organizations in extending adequacy and order in the broader areas of international administration, such as civil aviation, communication, finance, food and agriculture, health, labor legislation, and the non-self-governing territories, afford firm indication of what might be achieved were the problems of judicial administration to be attacked with comparable vision and vigor. Surely the resources of growth, hitherto discussed, could be vastly fortified. Here are matters for the attention of the increasing numbers who are giving thought to the improvement of the United Nations.

In the matter of extending law into new areas through recourse to international equivalents of legislation, there is probably less of need for the improvement of United Nations institutions and procedures and more of need for bolder recourse to the institutions and procedures which have been so well provided. Building firmly upon experience, it has been possible through the United Nations to bring the international conference as an agency for lawmaking by agreement to its highest level of efficiency up to this time. There will be none to suggest that perfection has been attained. It may be confidently asserted, nevertheless, that international conferences looking to agreement upon new law are now assembled more easily and expeditiously, that they are better organized and better prepared, and that their procedures afford more assurance of useful accomplishment than ever before. Where conditions appear less than ripe for one form of useful action, it has been found that there are other forms of useful action to which we may turn. Affecting favorably the whole of such effort, qualities of versatility, continuity, and responsibility have developed which, notwithstanding a persisting cumbersomeness, have given hopeful augury of yet more effective functioning. The emergence of these qualities has been less dramatized than the Security Council's frustrations, for example, but it is none the less real. On occasion there have been law-making conferences which would suffer no whit from comparison with a considerable number of the national legislatures. Here is a development which would appear to merit an even more considerate reflection than it has yet received. Reflection may well convince, as we have suggested, that it is not so much new agencies which are required as better use of the agencies at hand.

The reëxamination of objectives is a more elusive task which perhaps belongs as much to those engaged in research in universities or elsewhere as to those who are serving actively in the institutions of organized coöperation or government. It is something which requires broader horizons and more of contemplative effort than are ordinarily permitted the harried staff official or the instructed delegate. Nevertheless the United Nations appears to be contributing to a noteworthy progress at both the technical and the policy levels. Notably in the work of its specialized organs and its related organizations, the United Nations is expanding steadily our knowledge of the constituent nations, of the bases of their distinctive interests, and of the ways which may be opened to a feasible conciliation. In due course such knowledge not only invites but compels some reappraisal of objectives. There may be a good deal of trial and error in the process, but the trends are constructive.

There is evidence that transient frustrations at the highest level, so widely publicized, have had at least the incidental effect of shifting some emphasis to less spectacular but no less important work on the foundations of peace. What cannot be won today in the more dramatic contests may be won tomorrow by assuring broader and firmer foundations. In such tactical advance the grand strategy is affected. There is also evidence that agencies of the United Nations have been prompted by the tough resistance of realities to reach for variant bases of accommodation where uniformity or universality are presently beyond the grasp. Plans for the International Law Commission, formed to promote "the progressive development of international law and its codification," disclose something of this. The encouragement which is given in the Charter to regional adjustments has comparable overtones. Again, the grand strategy is affected. Certainly no period in the progress of international coöperation has evidenced so profound a concern for the rights of the individual. Here an earlier insistence upon reorientation has found its place in the Charter and is having notable consequences. Any implementing of such concern, needless to say, must continue and fortify the reappraisal of objectives.

This is not the place to project a discussion of the more embracing effort to prevent and remove threats to the peace on political, economic, or social fronts. The over-all enterprise is global. There have been successes in Palestine and Indonesia, frustrations in Kashmir and Korea, and elsewhere advances or retreats. Over all there is the dread specter of bipolar conflict. Where effort has succeeded, the opportunities for growth of the law have been extended and law has made its contributions to the stabilization of order. Where frustrations have been encountered, the law must await more favorable opportunities for an expanded service. Meanwhile, this much may be said with confidence. The old days of every nation for itself and God for us all are gone forever. If the institutions and procedures of the United Nations were to be destroyed today we should be obliged to recreate them tomorrow.

VI

Among our bolder thinkers and more forthright planners, there are those who are turning hopefully to projects for world government. In one form or another, world government has become the objective of an impressive pacifist movement since the second World War. For many it means that we should work through the United Nations, bending every effort and exploiting every opportunity, to transform the existing structure of organized coöperation into a United States of the World. Others would concentrate initially at least upon the federation of the Western democracies and as many more as might be persuaded to join. Others, still more ambitious, would project a constitution for all mankind. We shall not attempt to describe the varying programs to which various groups within the larger movement have become committed. The cause is urged in manifest sincerity and is supported by great numbers. Support tends to increase barometrically as the bipolar conflict worsens or as new super-weapons are projected. What shall we say of this movement and its relation to the struggle for law and peace?

At the outset let us concede that the world government movement is not something to be put aside brusquely as daydreaming or as a mere activity outlet for those who find it difficult to face the realities of life on this disordered planet. Its inspiration derives from too much of well-grounded dissatisfaction with the present and too much of intelligent hope for at least the distant future. Probably it should be conceded that it is not something to be put aside entirely whether brusquely or otherwise. There is always a place in healthy society for projects of betterment promoted intelligently, however impractical they may seem in the period of their promotion, and for the propaganda which keeps them astir in the forums of free discussion. Although they may appear to provide no more than a light on the far horizon, this does not mean that they are without utility. Most of us may be ill-fitted by temperament or capacity to tend the distant light and inclined to be correspondingly impatient with others better fitted. We should not let impatience obscure the importance of illuminated though distant horizons. Much of history is the narrative of an ultimate realization of ideas hopefully, though perhaps unrealistically, projected by the idealists of an earlier time. The more troubled the time the more unwise it becomes to put aside the idealists and their ideas.

If as much may be admitted, we should be ready for the appraisal which appears to be required by existing circumstances. Mankind needs peace and needs it desperately. Most of mankind wants it. It is acknowledged everywhere that law in some form is an indispensable means. In these essays we have endeavored to point up some of the problems and the possibilities. What are the propagandists for world government contributing?

It is suggested that the wiser heads of the world government movement are contributing usefully as gadflies of United Nations improvement. We should not belittle their service. There is a vast deal of improvement that is needed and feasible. We may hope that they will not become so completely absorbed in repairing deficiencies at the top of the structure—in attempts to restrict the "veto," for example, or to regulate armaments or create a united force—that they lose sight entirely of the things which need to be repaired or reconstructed nearer the base. A political peace as we may be able to obtain and keep it, by all means—but does anyone seriously think that we can keep peace over the years by political votes and armed contingents without more? That would be deceptive thinking indeed. Where political statesmanship is able to hold or gain, the law may advance. Let the protagonists of world government take note also that if law is to advance effectively there are foundations to be fortified and sturdier foundations to be laid.

As we have endeavored to show, the institutions and

processes of the law's administration need to be strengthened and improved. Law needs to be extended into areas which up to now have been a no-man's land of competing policies. The extravagances of sovereignty and their corresponding restrictions of the concept of "legal disputes" and exaggerations of "matters which are essentially within the domestic jurisdiction" need to be progressively mitigated. Always to be stressed is the basic proposition that it is the human individual rather than the inhuman state that is the subject of our ultimate concern. Propagandists for world government have already contributed a little to the illumination of these and related considerations. With better understanding they may contribute more. It is suggested that the reformists of the movement, at least, may do much to arouse and illuminate in the continuing struggle to assure that law and peace or peace and law move forward together on an ever expanding front.

It is possible that even the grandiose projects advanced by the more radical wing of the movement may have a little utility. Unlikely as it is that any of their projects will ever be seriously considered for adoption, they may help a little to point up deficiencies in the existing organization of coöperative effort. They may broach also some useful ideas for such parts of the world as suffer from a persisting political or social confusion. Plainly the recent war has left power voids in the world, conspicuously in western Europe and in parts of Asia, where strength will have to be cultivated and a balance restored through much firmer union among existing political bodies. The persisting anarchy of a disorganized area cannot command respect. It can only invite a dangerous maneuvering for advantage. Proponents of the grand design are not likely to be called in as consultants in such areas, but they may help to illuminate the way a little for those who are to be consulted.

Beyond contributions thus suggested, it is difficult to see much of immediate utility in the more ambitious projects. When presented as alternatives to what we have, they become positively harmful. Surely we cannot think seriously of loosening the hold on what we have in pursuit of the will-o'-the-wisp of a supreme parliament! Surely we may not hope to raise the ideal superstructure until foundations have been more securely laid! Peace and the good order must be built on experience. Order can never spring full panoplied from even the most inventive minds in conference or convention. These truths must be obvious. The way of experience may be hard but there is no other. If world government enthusiasts may become reconciled to these truths without too much impairment of their crusading zeal, there is no reason why they should not march helpfully in the vanguard of constructive effort.

VII

We shall conclude these essays with some comments upon the role of the United States in the struggle for law and peace. There will be none to doubt that circumstances have cast our country in a role of great importance. The sequence of events has brought the United States, whether it would or no, to a position of leadership in world affairs. Its influence in arms in the period of the late war was vastly significant. Aroused at Pearl Harbor, the giant came awake, commanded a willing and unstinted sacrifice, achieved an unprecedented mobilization of resources, reinvigorated its beleaguered allies, and went on to share a victory of global proportions. There are indications that its influence in matters of policy is becoming comparably significant, though a persisting gap between shifts of policy and the understanding of what the shifts entail compels some reservations. It is little short of amazing that a political isolationism so deeply rooted in history and tradition could have been so completely reconsidered as the war taught its harsher lessons or that the lessons, even in war, could have been absorbed so swiftly. It remains to be demonstrated that a revolution extraordinary in national outlook has been accompanied by mature appreciation of the responsibilities involved. Perhaps appreciation may come only with the unfolding of time and a more protracted experience.

The influence of the United States in matters of law, on the other hand, has been anything but impressive. There have been paradoxes of action and inaction, of boldness in preachment and timidity in practice, of one step forward and two to the rear. In recurring instances a forthright support of principle has been followed by manifestations of unwillingness to incur the risks which are clearly indicated. One wonders sometimes whether the habits of an isolationist past, so completely discredited in the realms of arms and policy, have returned to plague us in the less understood and less dramatic contests of the law.

It would appear that comment should begin with the removal of whatever lingering doubts there may be as to the capacity of the United States to wage peace as effectively through law as by force of arms or manipulations of policy. The United States has the required capacity. Historically it emerged in a peaceful revolt against the failures of confederation. It was organized prudently on federal principles. In a long experience which has included the trials of civil strife, these principles have acquired fiber and a mature significance. From it all we have learned that responsibility and the corresponding power in all that pertains to international affairs must be wholly national. There can be no division of responsibility in our dealings with other peoples.

The principles which have thus enabled the United States to take its place as a nation in the community of nations are in the original Constitution. The decision as to war or peace is there made the exclusive province of the national government. An acknowledged residuum of state concern has had no practical application of consequence, and as the national power is now organized and served it is unlikely that it ever will. The conduct of international relations, with its attendant formulations of policy, is vested exclusively in national authority. State concern has been vestigial from the beginning and even the vestige has declined steadily in importance. Treaties are made by the President by and with the advice and consent of the Senate, provided two-thirds of the Senators present concur, and less formal but no less obligatory agreements are concluded from day to day by the national executive in its conduct of foreign relations. The treaty power is necessarily and expressly denied to the states. All treaties made "under authority of the United States," like the Constitution and the laws of the United States made "in pursuance thereof," are "the supreme law of the land." The judges in every state are bound thereby, "anything in the constitution or laws of any state to the contrary notwithstanding."

Notwithstanding the forethought and wisdom of the framers so clearly expressed in the original document, the contemporary sources which have been so helpful in elucidating the details of purpose, and the progressive accumulation over the years of illuminating interpretations, there have been relapses from time to time into a curious kind of constitutional frustration. Of the earlier relapses some appear to have been inspired by a genuine doubt as to how to operate successfully in relation to other nations while retaining the federal distribution of powers within our own. Thus, when alien residents were injured in outbreaks of violence which state authorities should have prevented, the United States began by taking refuge in federalism and denying its international responsibility. If the national government was not internationally responsible, there was none that could be. Accordingly, it must be conceded in retrospect that the national denial was a transparent sophistry. Abroad it was generally so regarded. When our citizens were injured abroad, on the other hand, the United States tolerated no such retreats into constitutional incapacity on the part of other governments. Later the United States, while continuing to deny a strict legal accountability in such instances, nevertheless paid indemnities as an act of grace where indemnities were due. Eventually even this face-saving formula had to be abandoned and the United States came to respond externally as a nation among nations, without reference to internal difficulties deriving from its federal structure.

Other and more recent relapses appear to have been inspired less by constitutional doubt and more by sheer confusion and timidity. There has been discussion of a constitutional aspect, of course, as there generally is with us, but what else can we say in candor of the recent abdication of responsibility and leadership on the part of the United States in the matter of extending the compulsory jurisdiction of the International Court of Justice over legal disputes? We have commented hitherto upon the importance of this effort in relation to the more embracing struggle for law and peace. Here we must note that the United States has been consistently on the side of timidity. When the matter was squarely presented to national authority in 1946, there emerged such an emasculation of the projected undertaking and such an abdication of leadership as merits neither excuse nor apology. The United States accepted compulsory jurisdiction in relation to any other state accepting the same obligation with the express exclusion, among others, of disputes "with regard to matters which are essentially within the domestic jurisdiction of the United States of America *as determined by the United States of America.*" (Italics added.) What an acceptance! There had been previously no such exclusions in the declarations of other nations. Unfortunately there have been since a few acceptances in the contradictory and emasculating formula first put forward by the United States. If this be leadership, assuredly it is leadership in the wrong direction! No one will deny that there are risks in the acceptance of compulsory jurisdiction without reservation, but they are infinitesimal when viewed in perspective among the calculated risks to be assumed if peace is to be waged successfully. Commitments to adjust disputes by "peaceful means" and "in conformity with the principles of justice and international law" will hardly be implemented by such negations. The role of the United States in waging peace, no less than its role in waging war, requires courage and the calculated risk. Our country has great responsibilities and a corresponding capacity. As regards the matter here discussed, we can only say that thus far it has failed lamentably.

There have been still other relapses of late in which the retreat into an asserted constitutional difficulty is hardly more than a screen for the deeper internal cleavages with respect to commitments which considerable numbers of our people are reluctant to undertake. War and its ensuing unsettlements have made new commitments urgent. For the United States, as for others, the commitments have their price. Payments required now are nominal, but they might ultimately become more significant as precedents. Alarmed at the remote though conceivable import of such precedents, the over-cautious and inward-looking have found it less offensive to talk of the impact of precedents upon federalism than to face up squarely to the problems of minorities or social betterment with which they are really concerned. Thus, matters which are primarily matters of expediency have come to be debated in terms of constitutionality, though the constitutional progress of the United States has long since made such debate largely irrelevant. It is pleasanter and more plausible to talk of the federal distribution of power than of the lives and liberties which power may affect.

There is pending in the Senate of the United States at the moment a Convention on the Prevention and Punishment of the Crime of Genocide which was prepared in conferences of the United Nations. Does anyone who has read history even superficially feel anything but humiliation in recalling the weakness and futility of earlier reactions to such bloody business as this convention defines? Does anyone experience anything but profound shock in recoiling from the incredible but recorded brutalities of a modern dictator crazed with power? Should anyone who has studied with any care the history and text of this pending convention, with attention to its preparation and to its precise and guarded phrases, take alarm at its conceivable impact at some future time and in some improbable event upon some detail of the distribution of power between nation and state in the United States? International conventions are made to be implemented and applied by responsible and fair-minded men. This convention is not self-executing. The contracting parties undertake to enact the necessary legislation "in accordance with their respective constitutions." There is a guarded anticipation of but no commitment whatever to an international tribunal. Yet at the moment the debate in our country is more concerned with federalism than with genocide; and the prospect that the United States will soon take its place among the nations who are about to bring the convention into effect is not encouraging.

There is also in preparation at this time, in conferences of the United Nations, an International Covenant on Human Rights intended to implement as much of the Universal Declaration of Human Rights as corresponds substantially to those individual rights and freedoms which have long been secured in the written or unwritten constitutions of Western democracies, including our own. One must be isolated indeed who remains insensitive in the welter of these post-war years to a tremendous upsurge over the world of concern for human rights and freedoms. In the Universal Declaration, the General Assembly of the United Nations proclaimed "a common standard of achievement." The common standard embraces ideals of freedom which have become traditional in the West, and also ideals of economic and social betterment which have not been similarly associated hitherto in traditional Western thinking. It is not apparent that the association is harmful when presented in such generalities. It may be good. Those who recoil from even the generalization of ideals of economic and social betterment would do well to remember that most of the world's peoples have never had enough to eat, that they will need food in their bellies before they can appreciate civil liberties and the ballot, and that there is a virulent ideology at large in the world which is tempting them even now with promises of food without freedom. In any case no one has suggested seriously a practical implementing in the proposed International Covenant of more of the "common standard" than has been woven long since into the very fabric of our Western life. We prize the traditional liberties of our bills of rights. We commend them to other peoples. Why fear them in a treaty? Yet fear has become increasingly articulate in reaction, not to liberties as such, but chiefly to the possible impact of a proposed international accord upon our national organization of power.

The alarmists have noted, as they must, that there is no longer a serious constitutional question concerning the sufficiency of national power. The Supreme Court has affirmed repeatedly over the years that the nation's treaty power embraces, subject to limitations which are largely academic, "any matter which is properly the subject of negotiation with a foreign country." Moreover, as the same Court remarked in a famous opinion thirty years ago, while "the great body of private relations" usually falls within the control of the state, it is clear that a treaty may override state power. The national power which has thus overridden the states from time to time in matters of procedure, property, regulation of business, or the protection of migratory birds may assuredly operate as effectively with respect to human rights and freedoms. In the excitement of an extraordinary exaggeration of the threat to states' rights which is assumed to be involved, nevertheless, it has been seriously proposed that the United States should henceforth include in every treaty of law-making effect a provision that the treaty is not to alter the respective powers of national and state government within the United States! It has even been proposed that the Constitution of the United States should be amended to impose express limitations upon the treaty power, or to modify or repeal the clause which makes treaties a part of the supreme law of the land! These are counsels of exaggeration and fear to which we can ill-afford to listen. We have never withheld from our government the power to win a military victory. It would be disastrous if we were to withhold from it the power to win peace under law.

Elsewhere in these essays, we have commented upon the importance of law-making treaties in relation to the more embracing struggle for law and peace. It is enough to refer here to the earlier comment. Nor is there place here for a more extended comment upon constitutional aspects of the problems of power. They are important to us, of course, but on the larger stage and in relation to the more embracing enterprise their importance becomes incidental and relatively minor. Problems of policy are presented which we shall consider on their merits as they arise and which we shall resolve in the light of experience with a proper regard for constitutional tradition. Meanwhile the suggestion is renewed that if the United States is to share as it should in leadership it must be comparably effective in war, in policy, and in law. Otherwise we preach but cannot practice. Otherwise we befuddle ourselves and bewilder our friends elsewhere. Otherwise we become from choice a cripple in the waging of peace. These things we must see in full perspective and not narrowly. If we go on winning wars and losing the peace, we may find one day that there is no vitality left with which to win a war.

VIII

In summary, therefore, we must conclude that law and peace are not separable but are intimately related aspects of the same great enterprise. The good order which embraces both will be formed realistically of such materials as were considered briefly in the first of these essays. It will conserve whatever is good and useful in the system of existing law which was surveyed briefly in the second of these essays. It will exploit to the utmost all existing opportunities for a useful growth, and it will create new opportunities. In our time and as far as we can now see into the future, it will expand through an improvement and strengthening of the United Nations. Here it is worth-while to remind again that most of the deficiencies in what we have now are but varying aspects or phases of the disorder which is inherent in relationships so imperfectly organized. Where the world of nations still retains those features once so aptly described as characteristic of a state of nature, the deficiencies retain a disturbing vitality. Where more substantial integration has been achieved, they are less in evidence. In plain speaking, the struggle for law and peace is a continuing struggle to establish in the world an improved organization of mankind on bases of understanding and decency. That is the substance of the good order which we call peace. In simplest terms, that is the meaning of law. Believing firmly in right over might, in order under law, our own people would do well to reappraise their strategy of peace in reliance upon these simple premises. In order that simplification of premises may not be misleading, they should also remember that the peace front is as vast and complicated as any in war. Bold in peace as in war, there is no measuring the contribution which the United States might make in our own time.

Afterword

As the Foreword will have suggested, the scope and content of these essays were determined in February 1950 when the lectures were delivered. The text as it now appears was well on the way to completion when, in late June, the North Koreans swept southward across the thirty-eighth parallel in military adventure. Events of tragic consequence have since occurred in that country. What of their relation to law and peace? Although it is obvious that the time has not come when these events may be appraised in perspective, there are some observations, made timely by Korea's tragedy, which should provide appropriate matter for a relevant Afterword.

Surely there will be few who doubt now that power must be kept in balance pending the patient development of orderly equivalents, that weakness in this disordered world merely invites aggression, and that the demobilization of the forces of order and decency which proceeded so swiftly after 1945 was a costly and tragic error. This is not mere hindsight. There were warnings enough, though they were persistently disregarded. On the other hand, it must be equally and painfully clear that mere power, even the power of many in collaboration, is no assurance of an enduring order. Peace enforced with arms is war, and war, whether waged singly or in united action, is equally destructive of the material and spiritual resources of which the better society must ultimately be built. It used to be said at Geneva that the methods of organized restraint or coercion might serve in large disputes between small nations, and possibly in small disputes between large nations, but that they could not possibly succeed in large disputes between large nations. That is still true. Organized force for the coercion of great powers, without more, is an oversimplification. Moreover, it is a desperately hazardous oversimplification.

Notwithstanding the disastrous consequences of some earlier oversimplifications with respect to Korea, there will be those who assert that unless commitments to suppress aggression there are successful, come what may, the United Nations is done. No generalization could be more shortsighted or ill-founded. The United Nations is only beginning. The first article of its Charter pledges "effective collective measures . . . for the suppression of aggression." However valiant the effort made in 1950 by nations willing to honor such a pledge, we have to say that in a world so sharply and tragically divided the pledge could not be kept. History will ultimately place responsibility for that where it belongs. The same article of the Charter contains a further commitment "to bring about by peaceful means, and in conformity with the principles of justice and international law, adjustment or settlement of international disputes or situations which might lead to a breach of the peace." In that commitment there is clear indication of the long-term enterprise to which, on a more embracing front, the United Nations must be increasingly dedicated. The larger enterprise has been conceived in patience and understanding. It must be prosecuted with persistence and an unflagging zeal.

It should be observed also that the Korean affair has had its compensations, dearly bought though they were. If we have learned more of the perils of oversimplification on this complicated earth, we have also discovered a new unity of purpose among most of the nations and throughout the greater part of the world. Surely it is vastly significant that so many of the nations of the earth should have wanted peace enough to be willing to share the initiative in fighting for it and that they should have been willing to fight for a better order as their one and only objective. Such resolution may be rewarded some day with greater success. Meanwhile, if it can be further mobilized in support of the long-term enterprise to which the United Nations is dedicated, it may have a profound influence upon the whole structure and functioning of organized international coöperation.

As we progress, even in "blood, sweat and tears," we shall be increasingly mindful that there are no easy and simple solutions. The more enduring peace is not to be implemented in halting expedients, or bought with dollars, or even enforced with arms. Increasingly it must be waged in execution of a well-planned and an embracing strategy. Increasingly it must be waged with law. It is in progress thus conceived and persistently advanced that we may hope to glimpse such horizons as Whitman thought he saw in the twilight of an earlier interval of struggle:

> Years of the modern! years of the unperform'd!
> Your horizon rises . . .
> I see Freedom, completely arm'd and victorious and very
> haughty, with Law on one side and Peace on the other,
> A stupendous trio . . .

www.ingramcontent.com/pod-product-compliance
Lightning Source LLC
LaVergne TN
LVHW011817200926
848484LV00005B/1227
* 9 7 8 1 5 1 2 8 1 1 2 5 4 *